Rebel Hugger

A CROSS-COUNTRY JOURNEY TO SELF-LOVE, ONE HUG AT A TIME

MELINDA LEE

Table of Contents

To my Nana, who never got to write her story.

Preface

The first question people usually ask when they find out about My Year of Hugs, the time I spent a year hugging everyone I encountered, is why.

To me, it seemed simple. Hugs are an unspoken language of love and humanity, understood whether they're given or not. Hugs transcend beliefs, culture, and geography. Why wouldn't it be a natural impulse, to hug the people we meet?

So at first, I kept my answer simple: I hugged people because I wanted to share love. But after many radio, newspaper, and TV interviews, I began to understand that people didn't want that answer. It wasn't enough. It wasn't satisfying.

If humans weren't so complicated, though, that answer would be enough. Heck, if *I* weren't so complicated, that answer would be enough, and this would be the end of my story. But I am, and it's not. So here, my story begins.

Chapter One

When did I first learn I wasn't enough? Maybe it was at thirteen years old, when I was told by the other junior girl scouts that the only boy at camp didn't like me because I wasn't willing to let him touch my boobs. Maybe it was later that same year when for the first time a boy at school said he wanted to be my boyfriend—but only after he'd looked down my shirt. Still, those were just the first times I remember being aware of my inadequacies. The truth went back much further than that. I suspect that as a female, I had unworthiness encoded in my DNA.

I don't know if I would or could have addressed this core wound until the opportunity came in the form of a multiple sclerosis diagnosis—a chance at healing masquerading as a death sentence. I was twenty-four years old and while I'd heard of MS, I didn't know much about it. The strongest association I had with the disease was a TV ad for an MS medication showing a mother unable to hold her young daughter. That was seared into my brain. And so when my neurologist gave me the news, my mind flashed to that commercial. I sat in stunned silence, afraid to know the truth of what this meant for my future. Would I not be able to hold my own children?

My doctor told me inflammation had caused the wires in my brain to short-circuit. It would take time for one of two things to happen: either the inflammation would heal or my brain would rewire the short-circuited connection. In the meantime, he wanted me to get on medication and scheduled my first round of intravenous steroids for the following day.

The steroids were meant to aggressively halt the inflammation in my brain with the intention of limiting the amount of damage done. He also prescribed Copaxone, a daily injection, to fight the disease in the long-term and extend my life expectancy.

I trusted that he knew what was best for me because he was a doctor. I'd never known anything other than Western medicine, so there was no reason for me to think I had other options. I believed him when he said there was no cure for MS, and the best we could do was aggressively fight it to minimize its impact on my life.

So fight it aggressively, we did. And within three weeks after starting the steroids, I no longer felt the tingling in my body that had led me to the doctor in the first place. It was working! Until it wasn't.

One morning about a week later, I woke up with the knowledge that I couldn't speak. I hadn't yet tried, but I knew my mouth wasn't going to work. I lay in bed stiffly, afraid to move and willing time to stop so I wouldn't have to acknowledge reality.

I felt my boyfriend, Chris, stir beside me. I knew I couldn't face this moment alone, so I lightly shook his upper arm. He slowly blinked his eyes awake, a gentle smile greeting me long before he'd have woken up on his own. I tried offering up a genuine smile of my own to soften the reality of the situation, but something in my face must have given me away.

"What? What is it? What's wrong?" he asked.

I kept attempting a smile as tears dropped onto my cheeks. I just shook my head. It's all I knew to do.

Chris lifted one eyebrow, his forehead creased with concern. "No? What no? What is it?"

I held my left hand out flat while forming my right hand into a makeshift pen. I pretended to write.

"What? Paper? Can you not talk?" His concern gave way to fear.

I nodded, covering my face with both hands. I felt the bed shake as he jumped up to find a pen and paper.

When he returned to the room, I was still lying in bed and staring up at the ceiling, tears now streaming down my face and collecting uncomfortably in my ears. I sat up to grab the pen and paper from Chris's hands while questions flew from his mouth too fast for me to answer even if I could have spoken. "Is it the MS? It's not a stroke, right? Should I call the doctor? Are you in pain?"

I put the pen to paper and scribbled nonsense—apparently I couldn't write either. I knew instinctively it was the MS, but I had to wait for him to ask that question again so I could nod in agreement.

"It's the MS? Should I call your neurologist?"

I nodded again.

He put the phone on speaker so I could hear the conversation and respond to questions to the best of my ability. My doctor recommended another round of steroids, an outpatient procedure that involved a four-hour infusion every day for five days. With a plan of action in place, Chris hung up the phone and gave me a hug.

My limbs were shaking as I contemplated what all of this meant. Would I be able to work? How long would this last? Was there anything else that was affected? I looked at Chris and felt my heart swell with gratitude for him. I was determined to let him know. I opened my mouth and squeaked out an *I*.

With the saddest eyes I've ever seen on a human being, he said, "Don't. Please don't try."

I forced my tongue to the back of my teeth and exhaled an *L*.

"Please, stop." He turned his head away in what I hoped wasn't disgust.

I forced my lips into the shape of an *o* and breathed out again. The *ve* never quite made it.

Chris dropped his head, but I was determined. I again made the shape of an *o*, squeaking out an *oo* and accepting that this would be the closest I could get to *I love you.*

Chris wept.

* * *

My doctor treated the acute attacks with steroids, and I continued to take a daily injection of Copaxone. As with most prescription drugs, it came with a long list of potential side effects, but I trusted that my physician and Western medicine knew what was best for me.

One of the side effects I'd been told about was the possibility of a Copaxone flush—an immediate post-injection reaction (IPIR) whose symptoms included chest pain, accelerated heart rate, and breathing problems—but I still wasn't prepared for the swiftness of the heat that spread from my toes to the top of my head. My face was beet red, and my heart was pounding out of my chest. I knew the flush could last at least five to ten minutes, but after three minutes my anxiety took over, and Chris called for an ambulance.

By the time the paramedics arrived, the flush was leaving my body, although the anxiety that had come with it remained. Once I got a clear check on all my vitals, I felt foolish. I declined going to the hospital and apologized to the ambulance crew for wasting their time. The flush happened perhaps five more times, but since the doctor wasn't concerned, I tried not to be.

By the time July 2001 rolled around, the attacks (also called exacerbations) were showing no signs of letting up. I'd received nine steroid treatments—nearly one every other month. The steroids left me feeling lethargic, bloated, starving, and angry. My eyesight was deteriorating, and every time I completed a five-day steroid treatment, my body struggled with regulating my temperature, leaving my toes frigid but my forehead sweating. So when my doctor recommended monthly steroid treatments as a preventative, I was hesitant. "Are you sure that's the right plan of action?" I asked.

"Your MS is more aggressive than I expected," he said. "We'll only do it for three months. The other treatment we can try is Tamoxifen, but I'd really like to try the steroids first because Tamoxifen is a chemotherapy and runs the risk of infertility, and I know you and Chris are planning on a family. I'll prescribe you some oral steroids to taper you off the IV and help with those side effects."

"Oh. Yeah, I guess the steroids are the better option," I said, telling myself that my doctor knew best.

And it seemed he did. After more steroid treatments, I didn't have another attack for four months. That was progress! I felt as hopeful as I could, given the disease and its treatments were still ravaging my body.

Then, another two months later, vertigo hit. It was April, and I was taking a test in a night class at Western Connecticut State University. My head hovered over my paper, and I was in deep concentration when the entire room spun. I grasped the desk to keep from falling over and looked around desperately for a trash can I could vomit into. It turned out to be unnecessary, as the room righted itself within a second, but my heart didn't stop racing until I returned home safe from another spin. My next round of steroids began two days later.

By day two of my treatment, my body already felt depleted. As soon as I returned home from the hospital, I shuffled down the long hallway to my bedroom and climbed in bed to lie flat on my back. I'd learned long since to take the week off work when I was on the steroid treatments. Chris, now my fiancé, retreated to his man cave in the basement, where he worked from home on the large L-shaped desk of his own construction.

My body was as usual struggling to regulate its temperature. I'd gotten into bed feeling hot, so I'd left the covers off. But before long, I started shaking from the cold. I peered down at the end of the bed where the covers were. They looked so far away. I began to panic. How would I get them on me? I didn't think—no, I *knew* I didn't have the energy to reach down and grab them.

I needed to get Chris's attention. I urgently scanned my surroundings and spotted a coaster on the nightstand. I lifted my arm and swiped it. It landed with a dull thud. There was no way he could have heard that.

I began to panic. The only other thing on the nightstand was an orange elephant meant to be used as a paperweight but that I preferred to use as a decoration. I was terrified the delicate glass trunk would break, but I needed Chris.

I reached out with my left arm, but the elephant was too far away. I began to cry. It was too hard. Everything just felt too hard. I knew the only way I was going to be able to reach it was by raising my shoulder to give my arm a little more extension, but I was afraid to discover I couldn't do it. Left with no choice, I tried anyway. I felt the tips of my fingers graze the elephant and pushed with all my might. As the elephant fell to the floor, my shoulder flopped back onto the bed. I sobbed.

I heard Chris running up the stairs and yelling down the hall. "Are you okay? Is everything okay?"

I couldn't respond. I was too mired in shame. Shame that I needed his help. Shame that my body was so broken. Shame that I wasn't a wife who could take care of him, and that he had to be the one to take care of me.

Shame shouted, "See? You are nothing. Why did he even want to marry you? You aren't worthy of someone like him. You aren't worthy of anyone. You are a burden." It was a familiar feeling of unworthiness that had appeared long before my diagnosis.

Chris sat down beside me at the edge of the bed. My hands covered my face so he couldn't see my pain. Through my fingers, I gingerly requested, "Can you pull those covers up over me?"

"You just need me to pull the covers up?" he asked.

I nodded.

"Okay?" he answered questioningly. He gently pulled the covers up as far as he could with my hands still covering my face, then tucked me in around the edges—snug as a bug in a rug. He noticed the elephant on the floor and reached down to put it back. "Maybe we should get a bell or something?" he asked.

I nodded, still protecting my face from the vulnerability of being seen. He sat there for another minute or so, then quietly walked out of the room. I waited until I heard him back at his desk before continuing to sob as silently as I could. Finally, exhaustion overtook me, and I fell into a fitful sleep.

When I woke a few hours later, there was a glass of water by my bed. My body had recovered enough that I could sit up and drink. A few sips in, I remembered what had happened just before I'd fallen asleep and I felt shame make a resurgence. I couldn't shake it.

Needing to do something, my body moved of its own accord and lifted the covers off me. My legs dangled over the edge of the bed for a moment before my feet hit the floor and then began walking, step by slow step, toward the bathroom. My hands turned on the faucet to the bath.

I filled the tub, keeping the water at just above room temperature to avoid an MS flare. I slowly and gently lowered myself into the tub and felt my entire skin burst out in flames of pins and needles. I sank my head back onto the tub and let the tears mingle with the bath water. I was so tired I thought I'd fall asleep again, but instead tears began flowing faster and more furiously. Surprisingly, energy surged through my body—not in a way that I could use physically but in a way that set my soul on fire.

"This is not how my life was supposed to be!" I raged in my mind, my fists clenching at my sides in the resistance of the water. "This is not it!" I raged harder, lifting my fists out of the water and slamming them back down in a futile attempt to express the red-hot blaze threatening to explode inside me.

"This is not my life! I'm only twenty-six years old. This is not how I'm meant to live!" I yelled out, slamming my fists back down on the water again, not caring about the mess I was making on the floor. I clenched my jaw as I forced a guttural scream through my teeth. "This is not my life!" I loudly declared, knowing that moment would forever define a turning point for me.

I saw clearly two paths laid out before me. In the one I was on, I continued to follow doctors' orders and continued to become increasingly disabled until I found myself in a nursing home by the prime age of thirty-five.

The second path was hazy. It had no clearly defined steps toward a better future, but when I leaned in to the difference between the two paths, one thing was abundantly clear. This one had potential. I didn't know where that potential would come from. I didn't know what it would require of me. I didn't know if it would extend my time until I ended up in the nursing home to age forty or if it would allow me to extend the quality of my life to age eighty. I just knew it was the right path.

Faith wrapped me in a warm, cozy blanket of hope over the next few days, despite the fact that I didn't have the energy to seek out this alternate path and I didn't even know where to begin looking.

On my final day of arriving at the hospital to receive my IV steroids, I found a new patient sitting by the window in the seat I preferred. She had the privacy curtain pulled, which was fine with me. I'd just learned my favorite nurse, Pam, had taken a different role in the hospital, so I settled in for a long, lonely five hours.

About an hour into my treatment, my mom called. I don't remember the details of our conversation, but it must have been centered around MS because when I hung up, the privacy curtain around the window seat had been pulled back, and the new patient was watching me.

"Hi. I hope you don't mind. I couldn't help but overhear. So you have multiple sclerosis too?" she asked.

"Huh? Oh, yeah, I was diagnosed over two years ago," I replied.

"How's it been going for you?"

"Actually, it's been pretty aggressive. I've had ten exacerbations already," I said.

"Oh, wow," she commiserated. "That's a lot."

"Yeah, it is."

She hesitated. "I don't know if you'd be open to it, but I'd like to give you a business card of a nutritionist I've used in the past. When I followed the diet she prescribed, I felt the best I'd ever felt since my diagnosis. I'm actually pretty disappointed in myself for not continuing it. I'm planning on calling her as soon as I'm finished with my treatment."

"Oh, yeah, I'll take her card," I said as the nurses started detaching her from the machines. Her treatment was done. "Thank you."

"Will you be here again tomorrow?" She passed me the card that would change my life.

"No, this was my last day of treatment," I said, not knowing just how true that statement would be.

She wished me well, and I never saw her again.

I called the nutritionist from the cubicle of my part-time job the very next day. I stood, listening to the phone ring as I looked through my manager's empty, larger cubicle and out the windows to the parking lot. It soothed me to see a hawk streak across the blue sky.

"Hello? This is Dr. Karen."

"Oh, hi." I was startled she'd answered. "Yes, hi, I, um, I'm Melinda and I was given your card."

"Do you have MS?" she asked.

That was quick. "I was diagnosed two years ago. Someone at the hospital gave me your card and said you knew a diet that helped her feel better?"

"Have you read *The Multiple Sclerosis Diet Book*?" she asked curtly.

"No, I'm not familiar."

"Go buy the book and read it. It's by Dr. Roy Laver Swank." I clumsily gathered together a pen and paper in a rush. "When you're done reading it, call me back. Then I can work with you."

"I can't just set up an appointment?"

She sighed, exasperated. "Here's the thing. You'll need to give up all your favorite foods. You'll need to stop eating out. You'll have to give up ice cream, dairy, and red meat for at least the first year. No cheese. No desserts. No fast food."

"Oh, okay. Yeah, no. That's not for me, thank you." And I hung up. I'd tried giving up cheese for Lent once, and it was one of the hardest things I'd ever done. There was no way I was going to attempt that again. I got why she required that patients read the book before she'd agree to work with them.

Still, a seed had been planted. I thought about that rock-bottom moment on the bed when I'd needed Chris to pull up the covers. I had nothing to lose by just buying the book. It was a step in a new direction. That night, I searched the internet and bought the book that would forever change the way I thought about Western medicine.

By the time it arrived a few weeks later (this was in the days before Amazon Prime), I didn't feel ready to make any changes. But I was curious what Dr. Swank had to say, so I took a look. The first section of the book was devoted to his research. I could educate myself without it meaning I'd have to take action. I made a deal with myself that I'd just read that front section and then I'd put it away. I wouldn't ever have to look at it again.

I grabbed a blanket and some tea and tried to make myself cozy in front of the unlit fireplace in our front room. The oversize custom windows were foggy from broken seals, and I couldn't see much through them, but the natural light brightened the pages of the book.

Three hours later, I'd blown through the first two sections and had just arrived at the part of the book that described the action steps necessary to follow Dr. Swank's diet plan. I felt energized, hopeful. This medical professional had proof that his protocol healed MS patients, and why. I had more confidence in this book than I had in my own neurologist, who couldn't tell me why the medicines I was taking worked or what long-term effects they might have.

I decided to give the diet a try. It was simple, but it wasn't easy. Over the next few months, I had to learn how to cook, shop, and track what I was eating, all while maintaining a part-time job and managing the little amount of energy I had. I learned to swallow my pride and order grocery delivery (this was when it was mostly meant for the elderly). I learned to say no to going out to eat with friends. I determinedly said no to desserts, cheese, or a quick meal at a drive-through. I felt like I wanted to die inside, but my desire to heal outweighed this temporary sense of loss.

That first month was hard—a hell of a lot harder than giving up cheese for Lent—but I was determined. I remained so focused on the logistics of creating this healing lifestyle that I didn't even notice the effects on my body until that first month ended, when I realized I had more energy than I'd had since graduating high school ten years earlier. My resolve strengthened.

Every day, I continued to give myself a Copaxone shot, and the scar tissue built up around the injection sites in my arms, hips, stomach, and thighs. I wondered if I would run out of areas to inject. I wondered if it would even matter if the diet kept working the way it was. I decided to have a conversation with my doctor, Dr. Talesnik; I still leaned heavily on his expertise.

"Dr. Tal, do you think it's possible to run out of room for the injections? The scarring is getting pretty bad," I asked him.

"I haven't had that happen to anyone I know of," he returned.

"Okay." I trusted him, but my body was urging me to share what I'd been discovering outside Western medicine. "Dr. Tal? I've been following this diet by Dr. Swank, the MS Diet? Have you heard of it?"

"No, I don't believe I have."

"It's this diet he came up with to heal MS patients. It involves eating very low-fat and whole, healthy foods. He has decades of research and proof of its results." I spoke quickly, worried he'd tell me to stop and just stick to the meds he'd been prescribing. Worse, I was afraid I'd listen.

"Well, if you're asking if you can come off the medications, you'd have to spend at least an hour convincing me it's the right move. And even then I'm not sure I'd agree," he said, reinforcing the idea that he knew better than I what was best for my body despite the changes I could see and feel.

"No, no, that's not what I'm saying. I just wanted you to know that I'm following this diet and that I'm feeling pretty good," I said.

"Well, I think that's great. Keep it up." His words carried an undertone of lip service.

I kept it up. Despite the doubts of my friends and family members. Despite the emotional turmoil it put me through to decline most social engagements because they all revolved around food. Despite the extra time and energy the diet required that I didn't think I had but somehow found. I felt life returning to my body. I began to see a better future than the one I'd seen waiting for me when I needed Chris to raise the covers over my depleted body. I began to trust this new path I was on. I began to trust myself.

Three months later, I called my neurologist again. "Dr. Tal? I'm ready to come off my medication."

"Well. Okay. You remember I said you'd need at least an hour to convince me?" he asked.

"I remember. I'm prepared."

"Okay. Let's set up the appointment." And he patched me through to the receptionist.

Just as I had two and a half years earlier before my diagnosis, I confidently walked alone into the open elevator and pressed the button for the second floor to the neurologist's office. The first time I'd ridden that elevator, I'd been unprepared for the fate that awaited me. This time I'd already secured my own fate and was prepared to be the one delivering the news.

The elevator opened. I walked into the waiting room for the last time. I barely had enough time to open a gossip magazine to admire America's best-dressed celebrities when Dr. Talesnik came to personally usher me into his office. "Melinda," he said in his gentle, disarming voice. "You look good."

"Thank you." I smiled shyly.

"I understand you're ready to discuss coming off your medication?" he asked.

"Yes, I am." And I launched right into my rehearsed speech. "I feel better than I have in nearly ten years. Certainly better than I have while being on medication, especially the steroids. You know how badly they affect me. But it's not just the steroids; it's the Copaxone. It's creating terrible scar tissue at each of the injection sites, and who knows what other kind of scarring is happening inside my body."

I paused for a second to catch my breath, then launched back in. "Copaxone is still a relatively new drug. But the doctor who created this diet has decades of research that explains why the diet works, and it doesn't require me to place anything unnatural in my body. There are no negative side effects."

I had my doctor's attention, so I pressed on. "You aren't able to tell me why the Copaxone works because the research has yet to conclude why. You also mentioned that you don't know if there will be long-term effects because there are fewer than ten years of studies. Chris and I do plan on having kids someday, and there's no definitive research on the effects Copaxone might have on me or my baby. This is too great a risk to take when I feel so good on something that is completely natural and has no side effects to speak of."

I finished and took a deep breath. I knew I'd have to answer questions and I was ready to plead my case.

"I can't argue with any of that," Dr. Talesnik admitted. "I don't agree with your decision to come off the medications, but I can't argue with your reasons why you want to. I also can't say for sure which has had the greater effect on you: the medicine or this new diet. But I will say, I hadn't expected you'd still be able to walk into my office unassisted by this point, so the fact that you look and sound so great speaks volumes."

Tears filled my eyes.

"Despite my concerns," he continued, "I will support you as long as you agree to get an MRI every six months so I can monitor your progress."

"Yes! Yes! Of course, I'll be happy to!" After all, I wanted to monitor my progress too.

Dr. Talesnik gave me an uncharacteristic hug and wished me well.

Fifteen minutes later, I walked out the front door of the medical building that was witness to the death of a life I once knew and, two years later, the birth of one I chose. What I learned that day is that there's no need to spend an hour convincing someone of a truth that runs deep within you. The truth speaks for itself and emerges from your body in powerful waves of confidence and clarity. A force impossible to deny.

In fact, an MRI six months later would prove the scientific impossibility that my lesions were healing through the power of the lifestyle changes I'd made. In that moment, I declared myself the expert of my own body. I acknowledged that I knew what I needed more deeply and clearly than anything taught through a textbook. I no longer needed to rely on medical experts for the final say in what was right with my body.

I hadn't believed in my worthiness for years. But when I reclaimed sovereignty over my own body, I felt the first flutterings of an intelligence, an instinct, emanating from deep within. It was a small, still voice, and it said, "I know it sounds crazy, but this is the right path for us."

This is what I now call the Nudge. It had always been there, of course, but I first became aware of her when that other patient behind the curtain handed me her nutritionist's card. A lightness of being came over me that didn't waver even when I'd hung up on said nutritionist a few days later. The Nudge didn't desert me; she simply waited. Waited for me to be ready. She gently urged me to buy the MS Diet book. She lit up when I made the choice to read more about the diet. She poured confidence and certainty into me so that by the time I made my decision, I stood grounded, strong, and tall. No one could persuade me that this crazy idea wasn't the right one for me. I knew it was. The Nudge told me so, and I believed her. I didn't yet feel a complete sense of worthiness—I had years to go for that—but when the Nudge came calling, I found the beginnings of the worthiness that was my birthright and had been there all along.

It would take another nine years, one marriage, and two kids before I truly understood the power of the Nudge, that she was my inner compass, my north star, my innate wisdom. At first, she was difficult to recognize— quiet, unhurried, subtle—a stark contrast to the frantic, unsettled way of being I was used to. Every time I heard her, though, my body felt calmer and more grounded, even when the suggestions she made sounded absurd.

I was used to making fear-based decisions, but the Nudge invited me to make desire-based decisions instead. In this case, it was a choice between following the direction of my doctor because I was afraid of illness and following the direction of the Nudge because I desired wellness.

What made it hard was that I was more supported by others for my fear-based decisions. Yet any time I followed the Nudge's guidance, I felt certain everything would work out—and it always did. The same couldn't be said for my fear-based choices.

Slowly, I learned to trust the Nudge despite the judgments of others and recognize her more quickly when she spoke up. And so it was that when she came to call one random day in April suggesting a hug journey, I answered.

Chapter Two

When my youngest was old enough to stop nursing, time and energy opened up for me. I began feeling restless and I wanted to find something meaningful to do with my time. One night after putting the kids down to bed, I asked my husband what he thought I should do.

"What are you good at?" Chris asked.

"I don't know. I mean, I guess I like writing and I'm pretty good at that." I remembered gazing longingly at the books in the library as a child and wondering if one day my name would be on a similar spine.

"Have you thought about blogging?" he asked.

"Yeah, but I don't know what I'd write about. I don't really feel like an expert in anything."

"What do you mean? You're a mom," he said. "People are always wanting parenting advice and tips."

"I don't know. I don't feel like I'm that great at it. What kind of advice could I give that hasn't already been given?"

"Just talk about your life. Your experiences." Chris continued to make a case for blogging while I continued to argue all the reasons why I wouldn't be good enough.

I knew I didn't need to be an expert, but I wanted to at least feel like I had greater knowledge than the people who'd be reading what I wrote.

As if she knew just what I needed, our black lab, Sadie, came and rested her head on my arm, offering me a loving distraction. I looked around our drab media room with its beige carpet, slightly lighter walls, and black recliner chairs we chose to give the room a movie theater feel. Then my attention settled on the large, solid oak desk passed down from Chris's dad, who'd died the year we got married. I thought about my father-in-law's legacy as one of the people who helped start up *USA Today*. I knew I wanted to make that kind of impact on the world.

"I like the idea of blogging," I said. "I'll give it more thought. I'm sure I can come up with something."

For the next few days, I made the kids meals, cleaned up after their messes, brought them to the park, and ran to the store. All the while, the idea of blogging continued to tickle my brain. I debated writing about MS and my healing journey, but I hated the idea of giving my energy and attention to the disease that nearly took my life. While there might come a time when I'd want to, I knew this wasn't it.

I began researching mom blogs, but man, those moms really seemed to have their shit together. That just wasn't me.

I really wanted to write a travel blog, but that required traveling and I didn't know how that would work with a young family. Who'd help take care of the kids? Chris couldn't take off enough work to join me; would our marriage survive me being gone all the time? The more I thought about it, the less I thought it could work.

The tickling was driving me crazy, but I wasn't coming up with a viable topic to write about so I had to let it go. If I was meant to write a blog, an idea would come to me, but spinning my wheels trying to come up with something just wasn't working.

One day, as I drove past a local farm and rolled down my window to say hi to the cows and ducks, my mind wandered back to the tickle. This time, it wasn't asking what I would write about. It wanted to know what I was good at, just as Chris had asked a few days before.

Surprisingly, it was the Nudge who answered. "Love," she said. "You're good at love."

I chuckled. "Okay, but how does that help me?" I said aloud to the privacy of my car.

"You love big," she elaborated. "It's your gift to the world."

I wasn't getting it. Feeling a bit frustrated, I said, "Yeah, I do. But what am I supposed to do with that?"

The Nudge didn't respond with words; instead, she responded with warmth—a warmth that flowed from my heart and down my arms.

"Hugs. I freaking love hugs. You're right!" Excitement exploded through my body. I already knew what she was getting at before I could make sense of any of it.

"I could hug people. Oh, Oh! I could hug everyone I encounter. I don't hug nearly as many people as I did growing up in Connecticut and I miss hugs. If I miss them, I bet other people have their reasons to miss them too."

As I drove on, my mind spun. I could hug the mail carrier, cashiers, my friends, my neighbors. It might be kind of unusual, but if I did it as an expression of gratitude for that person being in my life even if for a brief moment, maybe it wouldn't be so weird. (I was wrong, by the way. It would definitely end up being weird but in an awkwardly joyful way.) The excitement continued to pulse through my body as the idea took hold.

"Oh my god, I'm going to do this!" I practically yelled out loud. My face fell as terror blasted through the excitement. This was the strongest message I'd ever felt from the Nudge, and I knew she wasn't about to take no for an answer. "Oh my god, I'm really going to do this," I almost whispered.

Then, before the terror could take hold and convince me what a terrible idea it was, the Nudge reminded me of my desire to write. Holy shit, of course. I could blog about this. It could be huge! I could hug people throughout the day for an entire year, then write about my experiences at night. It could be a way for me to virtually hug people who didn't live close by.

A year of hugs. My year of hugs. *Yes!* That's *it*! I could see it all as though it had already happened, even though I had no idea how that would come about.

Slowly the details formed as if in a dream, born out of that tickle in my brain. If I started on the first of May, that would give me a few weeks to prepare. But prepare for what? How? I didn't know. I figured I could start with checking out some of the blog themes Chris had sent me.

I knew I needed to let the idea take root within me before sharing it with anyone besides Chris. I needed to allow it to spread through me so that the fist of another's judgment didn't yank it out like a weed. So I protected it. Watered it. Fertilized it with plans, hopes, and imagination. When it felt rooted, it was time to strengthen it with the winds of judgment. I wasn't sure what kind of responses I'd get, so I started with someone I knew would at most create a gentle breeze.

Erin and I went to high school together, but we didn't get to know each other until after we'd graduated. She'd recently moved to Durham and was the only hometown friend I knew in North Carolina. Exactly one week after the Nudge dropped the idea into my lap, I called Erin from my car.

"Erin, I have a crazy idea," I said when she answered the call.

"What? What is it?"

"I've decided to hug everyone I encounter for a year and blog about it. I'm going to call it My Year of Hugs," I quickly spit out before I could change my mind.

"What do you mean you're going to hug everyone?" she asked.

I timidly explained my crazy idea to her. I was committed to it, but I knew that a strong enough wind could still knock it down. After I was done, I told her I planned to start in two weeks on the first of May.

I held my breath as she took a beat. "Why May first?" she finally asked.

I exhaled forcefully. "It's the beginning of a month. It's a nice, clean start date."

"No," Erin said, "I mean, why wait until May first? Why not start today?"

The embarrassment I thought I'd feel sharing this crazy idea out loud was replaced with calm groundedness as the Nudge let me know she agreed with Erin. My mind wasn't so certain. "Oh, I can't start today. I'm not ready," I said.

"Not ready for what? What do you need besides your own two arms?"

"I—I don't even have a blog yet," I sputtered. "Besides, I'm seeing my therapist today. I can't start on a therapy day."

"Are you kidding?" Her voice climbed an octave higher. "That'll make for a great start to your year. You'll get to blog about how your first day included your therapist!"

"Am I even allowed to hug my therapist? What if there's a rule against it?" I continued to push back against her suggestion despite the Nudge's insistence that we needed to start immediately.

"I guess you'll find out," she said.

I got quiet and contemplated my next move. In the pause, Erin spoke up. "Hey, I gotta go. You've totally got this. Call me after."

As soon as we hung up, I knew I was going to start that day. Actually, my body knew I was going to start that day. It felt terrified but also strangely calm. My brain, however, kept trying to persuade me otherwise. It reminded me of how awkward it would be to ask my therapist for a hug, convincing me that I wasn't emotionally ready—like I needed to be able to brace myself first before starting this journey, though I didn't know for what. But the knowing in my body was strong and wouldn't be swayed. Eventually my brain gave up.

That first hug was every bit as awkward as I thought it would be. It was surprisingly cold and distant, especially after I'd once again vulnerably bared my soul to her. It felt like she'd complied out of obligation, but whatever. I did it. I got that first hug.

When I arrived home, I sat down at the large oak desk in our media room and picked out the first blog theme I saw. I could always change it at a later date. Within thirty minutes, my first blog post was complete, and my 365-day journey had begun.

Throughout the journey and for years to come, unworthiness remained a constant companion, but following the Nudge opened doorways to new possibilities. When the Nudge invited me to discover a path to heal my MS through diet rather than Western medicine, I persisted until I was well. Yet I still believed it was the work of others who healed me; Dr. Swank, who created the diet plan, and my nutritionist, who guided me on that plan. I ignored the fact that it was the Nudge urging me on and that I was the one who relentlessly pursued that path until I was well. The Nudge wasn't deterred. She was determined to make my worthiness known to me. I just needed to hug a few thousand more people first.

Chapter Three

Once I embarked on My Year of Hugs (MYOH), the question I got asked most often after why was whether I was worried about my safety.

I understood the fear behind this question, but not once did I actually consider that asking for hugs might put me in harm's way. I believed in humans too much. I believed in their kindness. I believed in their capacity for making good choices. And I believed they were worthy of being loved despite their flaws.

I suppose I can blame that on my dad. Growing up, I watched him race out of the house to help drivers stuck on the road in front of our house because their car battery died or the small hill was too icy in the winter for them to make it. I watched him volunteer at the food bank on holidays, wearing outrageous outfits just to get extra smiles. I watched him volunteer to coach our youth softball team, then take the entire team out for ice cream at the end of the season regardless of whether we won or not. He'd chauffeur us in his dump truck so we could sit in the back and feel the wind in our hair.

I watched him stick up for the underdog and make sure we treated everyone as equals despite any physical or mental differences. He showed me everyone deserves kindness, and all it takes is a quick joke or bright smile, even when people aren't at their best.

The Halloween I was six, I was riding in the back-seat—not to be confused with the way-way back—of my parents' wood-paneled station wagon when the car came to a screeching halt. Some kids had egged our car. Dad jammed the station wagon into park and began racing after the young boys while Mom screamed for him to let them go. I imagine my younger sister, Bambi, was crying; she was only two and sensitive to abrupt changes. I turned my wide eyes toward my slightly older sister, Kim, who looked just as bewildered as I felt. We peppered Mom with questions: Where did Dad go? What's he going to do? Will he get hurt? What does it mean to egg a car? Why would someone do that?

Mom kept us calm by repeating variations on "he'll be right back," "he'll be fine," and "he probably won't even catch those kids."

I looked out my window to see Dad guiding a kid out of the woods. I didn't hear what was being said, but there was gesturing toward the car and the kid nodding his head in some sort of agreement. The boy was probably in his early teens, but he felt like a grown-up to me. I moved to the middle of the bench seat so Mom could sit next to me. The kid sat in the front next to my dad. No one spoke.

Dad drove us all to the nearest gas station, where he and the kid got out of the car, leaving the rest of us— well, me, anyway—wondering what was happening. Dad opened the back door and filled us in. "Hey, it'll be just a minute. This kid is cleaning up the mess him and his friends made, and then we're going to drive him back to where I found him. Isn't that right?" He directed that last question to the kid.

"Yes, yes, sir. I'm really sorry." The boy's voice quavered. I can now imagine what that kid must have gone through. My dad's a tall, strong, Italian man who maintained his imposing stature through the bricklaying work he did with his own father. Even people who knew his gentle nature were intimidated by him.

Once the car was cleaned, it didn't surprise me at all to see Dad gently teasing the boy until a smile of relief spread across the kid's face. Dad didn't hold anyone to standards of perfection. He knew we were all human and that humans make mistakes.

By the time I was starting out on MYOH at thirty-one years old, I knew firsthand not everyone was as good-natured as my dad. Heck, by that point even my dad wasn't as good-natured. But I believed the goodness in their hearts, even those who society might deem bad. I believed that circumstances could turn us away from that goodness, but that love would turn us back.

I didn't anticipate that I'd be tested on my belief in this almost right away.

Rather than pay for our garbage to be picked up, I routinely hoisted it into the back of my Ford Escape each week and drove it less than two miles away to the garbage disposal site. One day a few weeks into MYOH, my son Cooper and his brother Parker fell asleep in their car seats before I even reached the disposal site. I felt a little shaky, wondering if I'd have the nerve to ask a waste disposal worker for a hug. I rehearsed in my mind how it would go, part of me praying that no one would be available.

There was no line, and I backed right into my spot in front of the large container set down in the ground. An employee was sitting, barely contained, in an ordinary folding chair by the side of the container. He was my mark. He had long, curly hair with streaks of silver. It fully framed his face, blending in perfectly with his thick, bushy mustache and the beard that extended halfway down his chest. His eyes were dark and intense, staring blankly at the few cars passing in and out of view.

I got out of the car and swallowed hard, certain that I wasn't going to ask him for a hug. *Nope*, I thought to myself. *Can't do it. It's fine. I'll just ask the next time I'm here.* But on my way to the back of my Ford Escape, the Nudge piped up.

"You can't pick and choose who you're going to hug on this journey. You don't get to select who's worthy of a hug and who isn't. That's the whole point, to prove that we're all worthy. To offer kindness and love, especially to those who might not otherwise receive it. You've got to ask him."

But he has a smelly cigar hanging out of his mouth. Surely that gives me a pass? I countered in my mind.

"Ask him."

I slowly lifted the tailgate and dragged out one bag of trash at a time, delaying the inevitable. When I'd delivered both bags into the container, I lowered the tailgate and stood there for a moment, gathering my courage. I turned and let out a quick breath, then sidled over to where he sat.

"Excuse me?" I interrupted his blank stare.

He looked at me inquisitively.

"Um, can I give you a hug?" The question was out. I couldn't take it back now.

He quickly stood up and towered over me. I looked up just in time to see the smile reaching his eyes. He grabbed the cigar out of his mouth with his right hand, reached around me with both arms, and lifted me right off the ground, which startled me into silence. He was whole belly-laughing when he placed me gently back on the ground. "Anytime!"

I couldn't help but match his laughter with my own. "Thank you," I said with a big, goofy smile on my face. I really wanted to lessen my discomfort by explaining my reason for asking for the hug, but I didn't want to ruin the perfection of the moment. I didn't want anyone I was hugging to think I was only in it for my own selfish reasons.

"No—thank you!" he replied as I walked back to my car.

I was still laughing as I drove away, though I did my best to stay as quiet as possible so as not to wake the kids. I couldn't believe I almost didn't ask him. I'd judged this kind, loving, generous man because he looked straight out of a motorcycle gang—like being in a motorcycle gang precluded being kind. As I thought about it, I realized some of the fiercest, kindest justice seekers were in motorcycle gangs. It got me to thinking about other judgments I had. Where was I missing out on knowing an amazing person simply because of a preconceived notion of who they were?

Most of my life, I'd actually been accused of being far too optimistic, of seeing the world through a rose-colored lens. I was told I needed to get real, live in the real world, come back to reality. What reality were they even talking about? If the real world meant judging people and expecting the worst of them rather than the best, I wanted no part of it.

Something I noticed, though, was that those people telling me to come down from the clouds, the ones who judged entire genders and classes and races of people, were often able to connect on an individual level. The person who was loudest in condemning LGBTQIA+ people would turn around and become best friends with the gay guy at work. "Oh, not *him*," they'd say. "He's different."

That's kind of the point. You can't lump everyone together when you're giving a hug; they mostly happen one-on-one. MYOH gave me the chance to see that everyone has their own stories, and everyone's been through something. I got to experience each person as an individual apart from the label they chose or were given.

* * *

If I wanted to expand my hugs beyond my own family, clearly I needed to leave my house. During MYOH, I found reason to do so most days by going shopping, visiting friends, exploring a new park, going to the post office, or visiting a local farm. Often I ran errands just to come across someone to hug. And once, the opportunity to hug someone arose while I was driving.

I passed through the large intersection at Route 401 and Ten-Ten Road almost every day, and there would usually be an unhoused person there asking for spare change. On this particular day, I came across a man I'd seen many times before. He was short and petite with a youthful energy, but his skin was coarse and wrinkled and hung loosely from his bony arms. I couldn't tell if he was closer to thirty or fifty years old.

He walked slowly and with purpose beside the cars lining up to turn left. His smile lit up his entire face; he held a poster in one hand and made a peace sign with the other. As I approached the intersection, the light turned yellow. Without regard for the car behind me, I slowed to a stop before it turned red, rolled down my window, and reached for the five-dollar bill I saved in the center console for just this reason. "Hi! I said, slightly leaning out the window. "What's your name?"

"Butch," he grinned.

"No way—that's my dad's name!" I offered him the bill in my right hand.

"Oh man! This is what I prayed for! Just this morning, I prayed to God. I said, 'God, please let someone deliver me a five-dollar bill.' And here it is. He answered my prayer." His smile made his face an impossible degree or two brighter. His joy was palpable.

I knew I didn't have much time left before the light turned green, so I leaned out a little further and asked, "Can I give you a hug?"

He gave me an aw-shucks smile and leaned over for an awkward hug through the window. "This is what I prayed for. Five dollars. God answered my prayers," he continued to joyfully exclaim as he walked away. He didn't acknowledge the hug, but this moment wasn't about that for him. The light turned green, and I heard him in the distance shouting after my car, "God bless you!"

"Did you just give him money, Mommy?" Cooper's little voice piped up from the back.

"Yeah, I did, baby. He needs it. Did you see how happy that made him?"

"Yeah, he was real happy."

I hadn't given much thought to the impact this journey was going to have on the kids. Cooper was four, and Parker was only one. How much would they remember? How much would they take in? Was I doing a good job of setting an example like my dad, Butch, did for me? I knew I wanted them to see unhoused people as equal. Human. Worthy of love, belonging, and respect. I wanted them to live in my reality. The one where people aren't feared but understood. Accepted.

I received my answer only a few months later. Cooper was quiet and reserved, perfectly content to sit with a book in his lap for hours, even long before he had the ability to read. He was reluctant to approach people he knew, much less strangers. Usually when I hugged someone he maintained a grip on my pants or shirt while holding himself as far away from the stranger as possible. I think he was afraid they'd want to hug him too.

One evening when the sky was still too bright for street lights but dark enough that there was an eerie quality to everything, the boys and I were leaving a mega-sized Target. The parking lot was enormous, and I had a death grip on both boys as we walked through the lanes to our car. I noticed a man walking in our general direction but kept my head down. I just wanted to get home. I didn't think I had it in me for another hug that day, and the quality of the light had me on edge.

Just as I reached the car, he approached us. I didn't feel any threatening vibe coming from him, but I kept a grip on the boys as I lowered my defenses and turned to face him.

"Do you have any change?" he asked.

I sighed. "I don't have any cash on me, but I do have hugs to spare if you'd like one." I felt the words flowing out of me before I could catch them and reel them back in. Turns out I guess I did have another hug left in me.

He cocked his head to one side and checked my face to see if I was for real. I smiled and shrugged my shoulder.

"Yeah," he said. "I'd like that."

I dropped the kids' hands, knowing they'd grab onto my clothes as soon as I let go like we'd practiced, and reached over for a hug. I felt his head land softly on my shoulder for a quick second, and then he let go and walked away. My heart swelled. I reached back down for the boys' hands, but Cooper was looking up at me with an urgency in his eyes.

"Can I go hug that man?" he asked.

I felt an immediate impulse to say no, but just as quickly questioned it. I knew how to keep Cooper safe. I had no reason to believe this man would want to harm him. I was out there to prove everyone had a good heart. I felt I could trust my belief in that over my knee-jerk reaction.

"Sure honey, I bet he'd like that," I said. I walked Cooper over to him and watched my son get up the courage to ask him for a hug. The man looked at me for approval, confirming the goodness in his heart. I nodded. He reached down, and I watched with tears in my eyes as my little boy wrapped his arms around this man that he saw worthy of his affection.

I was conflicted. As a mom, was I doing the right thing? Would Cooper know to trust his own instincts and not automatically assume he was safe around everyone? I couldn't help but wonder if I was setting him up to be taken advantage of, but then, isn't that what everyone was concerned about with me? That I was too trusting? That I, too, would be taken advantage of? If the choice was between teaching him to be too trusting over not trusting enough; between living in the "real world" versus living in the clouds, then I knew I was doing the right thing. Life is so much more beautiful in the clouds.

* * *

By the time I hit the halfway mark in my journey, I'd proven to myself and others that safety wasn't an issue. People were showing up, just as I'd expected, with kindness, generosity, and love—even when the hug wasn't wanted.

I'll never forget my first no. I was at a Kroger in Raleigh without my boys and I'd had trouble finding my favorite tea. I asked a Black teenage employee for help. He kept pulling up his oversize pants as he walked me to the right aisle, found the box, and handed it to me. He was respectful and softspoken, and kept his gaze averted. I was simply grateful for his willingness to go out of his way for me, so asking him for a hug felt easy.

He looked at me for a quick moment with an expression I couldn't read. "No, thank you," he said and walked away.

I was dumbfounded. He seemed so genuine and caring, I was kind of surprised by his response. But mostly I was surprised by the casual way he delivered his rejection. Rather than feeling hurt, I was impressed by his awareness of his own needs and his willingness to put those first. He made me realize I might still have a lot to learn on this journey.

Since this experience, I've been tremendously humbled as I've learned more about my own internal biases. I can't possibly know what he was thinking or feeling, but it's ignorant of me to think the color of my skin didn't preclude him from wanting to hug me. May I continue to learn and evolve.

Chapter Four

I was taught to people-please. That meant prioritizing others' feelings over my own; showing respect, especially to the elderly; and giving out hugs even when my gut was saying, "Aw, hell no!" so I wouldn't hurt someone's feelings. Ironically the only times I found myself in potentially dangerous situations were when I was people-pleasing.

That year I spent hugging everyone I met, I joined the Friend in Deed program at the church I attended. Program volunteers brought church members to doctors' appointments when they couldn't drive, dropped off meals when they couldn't cook, and gave other kinds of support as requested. Simon, an older church member, had broken his hip and needed rides to physical therapy. I volunteered happily.

One particular Sunday, Simon sought me out after I'd dropped my boys off in child care, and we got to talking before the church service began. He mentioned an experience he'd had with wolves and a shaman out in the desert. It was just the kind of story I longed to hear. Just then the Reverend walked in, so Simon quickly suggested we go out for coffee sometime.

Alarm bells went off in my gut, but I didn't understand why. I genuinely wanted to hear more of his story, and I didn't want to be disrespectful and say no to this elderly man. I looked at him leaning heavily on his cane and wondered what in the world would be so wrong about agreeing to go. I told myself I was being ridiculous and I told Simon I'd be happy to meet him for coffee.

We made arrangements to meet at a coffee shop about twenty minutes from my house—by this time, Simon was driving again, so he could get himself there. I'd never been to this particular place, but we'd be out in public, and I figured I'd be fine. I still had concerns, but I never expressed them to anyone, not even Chris. They felt unfounded and silly. I just kept thinking about the wolf story and how much I wanted to hear it.

My stomach flip-flopped the entire drive to the coffee shop while I tried to convince myself I had nothing to feel uneasy about. I intentionally arrived early to scope things out, and as soon as I walked into the shop, my sense of unease grew. The dimly lit atmosphere, soft couches, and dark corners that would normally feel like a cozy blanket in a public space felt sinister instead.

I slowly walked up to the counter, ordered a mocha latte, and while I waited, craned my head to find the most visible place to sit. I heard my name called from a distance. Turning toward the seating area, I sucked in a deep breath. There was Simon, staring at me from a loveseat in the middle of the room. He raised his hand in greeting.

The room suddenly seemed much smaller, and I felt even more unsettled. When the barista called out my order, I grabbed my coffee and readied myself. So much for my early arrival. I walked over to Simon, gave him a quick hug, and sat as far away from him on the loveseat as I could without perching myself on the arm. I put my coffee on the table in front of us, subconsciously freeing my hands in case they were needed.

Simon moved in closer.

I swallowed loudly. No part of me even considered that it might be okay just to offer some lame excuse and book it out of there as fast as possible. Instead I plastered a smile on my face and continued playing the part of the cooperative girl. "So, Simon, I'd love for you to tell me that story about the wolves you mentioned at church."

He stared at me with beady eyes through his glasses, gave me a tight smile, and redirected the conversation to me, asking about My Year of Hugs.

At this, I settled a little. Talking about the hugs brought me joy, so I focused on that emotion and shining a light on the people I hugged. I was strategically keeping his attention off me as much as possible. When I wrapped up, I asked again about the wolf story. It was the sole reason I'd agreed to meet him.

He paused, just looking at me, and I shifted uncomfortably. With his arm along the back of the loveseat, he was almost close enough to touch me. I tried to imperceptibly back away but had nowhere to go.

After a very tense moment, he spoke again. "You know, Melinda, I was surprised when I heard you had a husband. I felt a strong connection between us from the moment we met." His tone was confidently suggestive.

Any part of me that was still in my body fled. My mind wasn't yet familiar with the term *disassociation*, but the rest of me sure as hell knew what it was. My eyes widened; I was frozen in place. I didn't hear a word of what else he was saying. My body just kept feeling *danger, danger, danger* while my mind was wondering what the hell was happening. The wolf had cornered its prey.

After a few minutes of trying not to take in his wildly inappropriate suggestions, my presence of mind returned to me enough to speak. "I'm not sure what you're saying, but I have to go. This is not okay," I muttered, using the harshest words my people-pleasing self found acceptable to speak aloud.

I picked up my coffee and my purse. Simon tried grabbing my hand to stop me; he was still talking. My ears felt like they were filled with cotton, and his words weren't penetrating. I pulled quickly away, walked to the trash can to throw out my untouched cup of coffee, and left.

I desperately wanted to drive away as fast as possible, afraid he'd follow me out into the parking lot, but the minute I got in my car, I began crying so hard I could barely breathe, much less drive. Instead I locked the doors and let myself wail.

How could I be so stupid? What the hell did I do to make him think it was okay to talk to me like that? Why do I feel so gross? How did I lead him on? What is my problem? Why didn't I listen to myself and the warnings I was receiving all morning? This is laughable, why can't I find the humor in this situation? What did I do wrong? What the actual fuck? I need to call someone. I can't call Chris. I can't tell him. What if he blames me for putting myself in this situation? Why did I put myself in this situation? I should know better. I should've heeded my suspicions.

I berated myself for a full five minutes before finally calling my mom. "Mom, I don't know what I did wrong," I cried to her. "He's old, and I met him in church. How did I get it so wrong?" As I explained what happened, I felt like a little kid again. My brain replayed all the times I'd put myself into situations that had left me feeling powerless and afraid.

She murmured all the things a mom's supposed to say about how it wasn't my fault, that I hadn't done anything wrong. It was comforting but didn't change my feelings of shame that said otherwise.

It was then that my stepfather, Gary, spoke up. I hadn't realized he'd been listening. "You know, Melinda, just because someone goes to church and believes in God doesn't automatically make them trustworthy."

My tears dried almost instantly. This was an obvious point but one I hadn't considered. I thought I knew the people I needed to avoid to remain safe, but this hug journey was flipping that on its head. I was just beginning to see that the people I might have once thought dangerous could be full of love and kindness, and that those who preached love and kindness were also capable of harm.

I realized that I was the only one capable of keeping myself safe—and that safety had nothing to do with a person's looks or what they believed. My ability to discern was there in the insistence of the Nudge. She wasn't just guiding me toward exciting adventures, she was also the alarm bells going off in my gut that warned me away from danger.

* * *

My relationship with the Nudge continued to develop, but it took time. It would be eight years after I completed MYOH when I finally understood a fundamental truth about her after spending the night alone with a stranger named Josh. It was, in fact, the exact opposite of what happened with Simon.

In 2019, seven years after MYOH, I embarked on a solo cross-country trip in which I stayed with family, friends, and strangers to build a global community one hug at a time. I asked my hosts for a place to sleep, a meal to eat, good conversation—and, of course, a hug.

Josh's house was one of my stops, but he texted me while I was on the road with a few questions before he agreed to host. I wondered if his concerns were less about the questions he had and more about gauging my reaction to his disclosure that he had Tourette's Syndrome, a nervous system condition that involves uncontrollable repetitive movements and/or sounds. Apparently I passed the test because shortly after our conversation he sent me his address and confirmed my stay.

Josh was the only single man I stayed with on that trip. As much as I believed in my fellow humans, I was also aware some situations required more cautious attention. After I parked on the street in front of his house, I opened Facebook and reread a friend's message sent after I'd confirmed my stay with Josh: "Oh yay!!! I'm so glad! And jealous!" I trusted Michele with my life. If she was this excited over my getting to spend time with him, he must be someone she trusted.

Despite the faith I had in Michele's judgment, I rehearsed in my mind what I might say, where I might go, and what I might do if things got uncomfortable and I needed to leave. I then spent another few minutes in my car, delaying the inevitable awkwardness of spending the night with a man I'd never met.

Finally I draped a bag over my shoulder and grabbed my suitcase out of my Ford Escape, Sally. I rolled the suitcase across the street and up the sidewalk to his door, where I rang the bell. I didn't have to wait long; Josh was expecting me.

The narrow house was dimly lit, making Josh's height of 6'7" feel even more intimidating. He'd playfully teased that he'd likely be the tallest person I'd hug, possibly ever, so I was prepared. But being prepared for something and experiencing it are two different things. After walking inside his home, I let go of my suitcase and dropped my bag so my arms were free. He leaned over, and I clumsily reached up for the introductory hug.

"Do you mind if I light some candles and turn off the lights?" Josh asked. My brain began flashing a danger sign until he quickly continued, "Artificial light bothers me and sometimes flares my tics, so I prefer to keep it dim with natural light. But if that makes you uncomfortable, we can leave the lights on."

My brain calmed some. What he said made sense and honestly, it sounded kind of nice. I hadn't yet noticed that my body didn't register danger even though my brain had. "Oh, I don't mind," I said. "I think candlelight will be nice."

I put my bags by the couch in his sparse living room while he lit the candles, most of them on the mantel of an unlit fireplace. Their flickering glow gave a warmth to the room, which contained only a couch and a coffee table on bare hardwood floors. When Josh finished lighting all the candles, he invited me through another dark room, past a grand piano, and into the kitchen. The small stove light was enough to show me this room was as stark as the living room.

He directed me to the seventies-style metal table in the middle of the room with chairs as uncomfortable as they looked. "Do you like spicy foods?" he asked. I thought it was a little late to ask that question, seeing as how it smelled like the meal was already done, but he clarified, "I mean, how spicy do you like it? I can add a little more heat to it if you'd like."

I glanced up at his face, expecting to be disappointed by the hint of an inappropriate suggestion thinly veiled as a joke. I was used to the men in my life viewing me as a sex object first and a human second. I was surprised to find no trace of a hidden meaning. "Actually, I like hot, spicy food," I answered.

Josh kept a seemingly intentional, respectful distance, which made me think he was very aware of the single man/married woman dynamic of this sleepover. I felt my brain relax even more, matching the ease my body had maintained. He scooped soup into two bowls and placed them at the table, went back for a few slices of bread, and then joined me. He asked why I was on this hug journey, and I explained my desire to spread love and acceptance.

Sharing my story often led people to lay down their armor and open up to me, and he was no exception. We talked about things I'm not at liberty to share, nor would I want to. They were his stories, and I was astounded by his strength in overcoming them.

In the spirit of being vulnerable, I asked if it would be okay to learn more about his Tourette's Syndrome. We'd finished dinner, and he stood up, grabbed our bowls, placed them in the sink, turned out the stove light, and then—without explanation—walked out of the room.

I wondered if I'd offended him.

He returned a moment later with a book in hand. "You can read a lot about it in this." He handed me the book, and I looked at the cover. *The World's Strongest Librarian*. By Josh Hanagarne.

"Oh wow! You wrote this?" The hardcover was heavy in my hand.

"Yeah." He talked on, giving me a glimpse into the book and his world. He told me that intense exercise helped exhaust him enough to limit the number of tics he experienced, and how this had led to him competing in strong man competitions.

"Do the tics hurt?" I asked.

"They can. But the worst part is not getting a break. My muscles feel like they're always twitching, and I'm constantly moving." The pain and sadness had left a permanent downturn to his eyes that made me want to cry, not because I was sad for him but because it was apparent that he'd turned his pain into something hauntingly beautiful.

When he was all talked out about Tourette's, he asked me to join him at the piano we'd passed earlier. I sat down on the bench while he lit more candles in what appeared to be a dining-turned-music-room. I noticed a guitar and music books, and the lack of a table.

"Do you want me to play a song for you?" he asked, sitting down next to me on the piano bench. I eagerly agreed.

"This is for you," he said.

His long fingers elegantly flowed across the keys, enveloping me in an enchanting melody like an extension of the hauntingly beautiful pain I'd caught a glimpse of earlier. He began to sing, composing lyrics on the spot that described me and my life—a life I had yet to share with him—with an accuracy that both warmed and unnerved me. For perhaps the first time, I felt truly seen and known. I wondered how this was possible when he knew relatively little about me. I knew I should have felt disturbed; instead, I was entranced.

When he finished, I begged him to record the song and send it to me. He'd captured the greatest parts of my essence so perfectly that I needed this reminder of who I really was because all too often I forgot. He smiled coyly. "I'll think about it," he said.

I knew right then I wouldn't receive a recording. It wasn't meant for posterity; it was meant for the magic of the moment. I closed my eyes and did my best to memorize the way I was feeling—the expansion of my heart, the glow of my own breathtaking beauty, and the breadth of emotion I didn't know it was possible to feel. I heard him get up from the bench we shared and pick up the guitar. The twang of the strings jolted me back to his music room and left me breathless, wondering what spell I'd just been under.

After an undetermined amount of time listening to him strumming the guitar and talking about his music, we retreated to the living room, where he'd left some sheets for me to sleep on. "You know, I don't really sleep much, so you're welcome to sleep in my bed. It's much more comfortable than the couch," he offered innocently. I truly believed I'd be able to trust him not to overstep any boundaries if I agreed to that sleeping arrangement.

"That's generous, but I think I feel more comfortable just staying out here on the couch," I said. I'd spent so long dissociated from my body that I couldn't recognize the feelings welling up inside me. He nodded in understanding. Without the need to acknowledge that our night wasn't over yet, I moved the sheets to the floor, and we both sat down on the couch to continue our conversation.

It was here that I invited him in to more details of my own life, sharing the overwhelming love I felt for my two boys and the frustration I felt in not yet finding my purpose in life. I'm certain he had tics throughout the night, but for the life of me, I can't remember any details of them.

As the night continued on, our deep conversation ebbed and flowed with ease. He listened to me in a way that felt like he'd been waiting his whole life to hear what I had to say. I didn't know if what I felt was attraction. I wouldn't have acted on it anyway, but I sure didn't want the evening to end.

Sometime after midnight, my eyes finally began drooping, and he took the cue. After helping me make up the couch, we hugged goodnight. Despite wondering if I'd ever be able to fall asleep after such an intensely captivating night, I immediately drifted off.

I often think about all that I would have missed that night if I'd listened to the objections of my brain as opposed to the relaxed sensations of my body. Would I have agreed to stay with him? Would I have judged his Tourette's Syndrome a deterrent? Would I have thought it too inappropriate to be married, traveling alone, and staying with a single man? Maybe. And I would have missed out on one of the most incredible people I've ever met.

Perhaps more importantly, I would've missed the opportunity to notice the wisdom of my body. A wisdom that far exceeded the intelligence of my brain, which had practiced people-pleasing for so long it didn't remember how to put me first. In that moment, I truly understood; the Nudge spoke from inside my body. I'd just spent so much of my life dissociated from it, I forgot she lived there.

Chapter Five

The terrible experience I'd had with Simon at the coffee shop showed me the places where I still needed to grow: mindset and boundaries. Mom tried to soothe me after Simon made that inappropriate pass, but her focus had remained on me. I'd felt comforted but still victimized. It wasn't until Gary, my stepdad, shifted the focus from me to Simon that I'd felt empowered.

After acknowledging that even people who go to church can be harmful, Gary had followed up with, "It wasn't okay that he did that. He was in the wrong."

How different that felt compared to when my mom said, "You did nothing wrong; it wasn't your fault." It's a difference I've thought about often while healing from other situations in which I've felt powerless. The intention is the same, but the emphasis isn't. It made the difference between feeling soothed and feeling free of the situation.

My hands were shaking, but my resolve was strong when I sent an email to Simon letting him know he'd made me uncomfortable and I wasn't interested in continuing any contact with him outside or inside of church.

* * *

Boundaries weren't a new concept to me. They were the reason I always asked before hugging people. I knew how to respect the boundaries of others. What my people-pleasing self didn't know was that I also had the right to establish boundaries for myself. Learning to do this felt necessary but terrifying. What if I offended someone? What if I lost friends? What if creating boundaries for myself left me all alone?

"May I give you a hug?" That was how I approached nearly every person I hugged during MYOH. I thought it would be not only weird to randomly approach a stranger with my arms out but also incredibly violating. In my view, everyone had their own dance space, just like in *Dirty Dancing* when Patrick Swayze taught Baby how to dance. He had Baby hold out her arms in a circle in front of her body and said, "This is your dance space." Then he said, holding his arms out in a circle in front of his, "This is my dance space." He told her that these personal spaces must be respected and entered only with permission.

This made sense to me, the idea of personal space. But perhaps it was obvious to me only because I had firsthand knowledge of what it felt like to have my space disrespected, even violated.

As a kid, I was often told I was wise for my age. I was also told I was too shy and sensitive, in a way that let me know these were bad things to be. I took that criticism to heart. When my parents asked me to give family members (or friends of the family) hugs, I did it regardless of how uncomfortable it made me feel because to do otherwise was being too sensitive. I needed to consider how they would feel if I didn't hug them, even when I was just three or four years old. It wasn't that I didn't want to hug any of my family members. It was that I didn't want to hug certain ones. Some of them, I just didn't know well enough. Others gave me an ick feeling. But I was determined to be a good girl and do as I was told.

When I was nine, my parents became friends with a woman from the Catholic church we attended. Late one evening when she was visiting, I dog-eared *Tiger Eyes* by Judy Blume and walked toward the kitchen to get a glass of water before hugging my parents goodnight. Cindy was sitting at the head of our dining room table talking with my parents. I'd met her once before and although I didn't know her well, I felt uneasy around her. I assessed the situation. Would it be possible to hug my parents without hugging her too? I didn't think I could. After all, she'd feel left out, wouldn't she? I didn't know why she made me so uncomfortable, but I really didn't want to hug her.

Determined to maintain my good girl status and show I wasn't too sensitive, I slowly walked up to my dad and gave him a goodnight hug. Shuffling my feet, I moved on to my mom and hugged her. Dragging my feet at this point, I walked with my head down to Cindy, gave her a quick hug, and retreated as fast as I could to my bedroom saying, "Good night, I love you" to my parents but in the general direction of the dining table so Cindy would feel included.

As I retreated, I overheard, "Oh my gosh! That was so nice! You've got a really sweet girl there." A smile bloomed across my face because it seemed I'd made the right choice.

It wasn't until years later that I learned she was physically and emotionally abusive to someone my family loved. I couldn't have known that at nine years old, nor could I have known that it was my much-criticized sensitivity picking up on something no one else was aware of. It was that same sensitivity that would one day help me discern where my boundaries were needed. But back then, I had no one to teach me.

During MYOH, requesting a hug was my way of offering people time to connect with their own experiences of sensitivity. I wanted to make sure they felt I was a safe person before agreeing to hug me.

The people who were most skeptical were some of my favorites. One day, I was in the checkout line at Kroger waiting for my groceries to get rung up and gathering the nerve to ask the cashier for a hug. Her curly black hair was pulled tight into a small ponytail with a few wisps fanned out at the edges of her hairline. Her face had a hard edge to it, and I could feel the solid walls built around her heart. She kept her face down and didn't engage in any of the small talk I offered.

This is a bad idea, I thought. *She clearly doesn't want to be bothered. She just wants to do her job and leave.* But I wasn't doing this hug journey to predict what people were thinking or feeling. I couldn't have even if I wanted to—I wasn't that sensitive. After I finished paying, I pushed my cart filled with my groceries and my sons to the end of the lane. "Before I leave, can I give you a hug?" I asked awkwardly, keeping my energy as vulnerable and open as possible while I walked slowly back toward her.

Keeping her body facing the next customer, she turned her head, looked back at me, and gave me a side eye. "Why?" she asked, skepticism and mistrust dripping off her tongue.

"Because I like hugs and I'm grateful for you today," I shrugged, deepening my vulnerability. I kept to my agreement not to share the story of my hug journey in order to respect the integrity of the love and gratitude being offered.

She continued to give me that skeptical side eye but opened up her left arm for a one-armed hug. I always tried to meet people where they were, so when I was offered a one-armed hug, I usually matched it with one of my own. But in this circumstance, I leaned in fully. I embraced her warmly with both arms.

I felt her meet my embrace as her right arm wrapped around me and squeezed just a little tighter. We both let go simultaneously, and when I pulled away I had just enough time to see the tear squeezing out of her eye as she turned back to her next customer. Maybe the walls around people's hearts aren't as solid as we think.

Moments like that kept me going throughout the year. Not just for the emotional release I saw when tears filled their eyes, but also in the physical way their defenses relaxed. It was incredibly fulfilling and emotional every time I got to witness someone drop their shoulders, settle in to their body, and take a deep breath after our hug. I saw that, if only for a few seconds of their day, they found some peace and connection. It made my sensitive little heart joyful. Surprisingly, it made that sensitive little heart just as joyful when someone did say no and respected their own boundaries. It let me see what was possible.

* * *

Shortly after receiving my first no from the boy at Kroger who helped me find my tea, I began establishing more of my own boundaries. I said no to PTA and bake sales because I wasn't the type of mom who enjoyed that sort of thing. I told Chris I wouldn't be responsible for his relatives' birthdays, that it was hard enough to remember my own. I asked Chris to start making more of the family meals because I ate so differently than he and the boys did, since I was still continuing to focus on maintaining the health of my body. I placed my phone on silent at night and removed as many alerts as possible so I wasn't bombarded all day long.

I felt good. I felt proud. I was becoming a pro at setting boundaries, or so I thought. I was wrong.

As I mentioned earlier, my second hug journey was a cross-country trip. The Nudge dropped the idea into my lap just as it had with MYOH. I'd started writing a book about that hug journey, printing out all of my blog posts from that year to review them, when I felt a sudden urge to meditate. (This doesn't happen to me, lest you think I'm some great yogi. I'm not.) At the time, I was a caregiver for a special needs dog, Bella, and it was nearly her nap time. I placed her carefully onto her mom's bed and tucked her in with some blankets before sitting upright next to her with my back against the headboard. Before I had a chance to settle in, Bella's sibling, Nala, jumped up and fell alongside my legs, her solid frame pinning them down. Sighing, I resigned myself to this less-than-optimal position and set a timer on my phone for a one-hour meditation (again, not typical).

I lay my hands face up in my lap and began taking deep, long breaths. My mind whirred a thousand miles a minute, attempting to distract me with thoughts of the book I wanted to write, the tasks I still had left to do for both Bella and Nala, and the shaming thoughts that reminded me of all the things I was doing wrong in life. I let them come and watched them go. Let them come and watched them go. Let them come and watched them go. Eventually, stillness appeared. In that stillness, the Nudge found its opportunity.

"It's time for a new hug journey," she said.

I mistook the Nudge for one of the mind-whirring thoughts and ignored it.

"It's time for a new hug journey and it's time to do it bigger," she emphasized.

This time I noticed the difference in tone and quality of thought. This wasn't anything coming from my mind. I watched the thoughts with curiosity.

"What if you traveled the country hugging people? I bet you know enough people on social media who know enough people to stay with along the way," she continued.

Excitement began stirring from deep within. I kept listening.

"You could build global connection one hug at a time, starting with the United States. You've always wanted to drive cross-country. This is your chance," she said.

My excitement grew, and I sat still for as long as I could before the fever of a new journey took hold. My eyes shot open, and I looked over at my phone. Twenty minutes. I'd lasted twenty minutes, but in that twenty minutes a new adventure was born.

My mind began whirring again, only this time its only focus was the new hug journey. The details needed for this journey flowed to me with ease. The Nudge offered me a deep knowing that this idea wasn't only possible but inevitable. "Oh my god, I'm really going to do this," I said, the same way I had when the first hug journey idea took hold. Chills ran through my body.

This was toward the end of August. I left for the trip a little over a month later at the end of September.

My intention for the cross-country trip (which I dubbed One Hug At A Time or OHAAT) was just as the Nudge had said: to build global community one hug at a time. Hosts of my adventure would offer me a place to sleep, feed me, and engage me in conversation. It was an opportunity to really get to know the people I was hugging, which I hadn't done in MYOH.

I didn't consider that it might also offer an advanced lesson in my continuing education on boundaries.

* * *

I was about a week and a half into my four-week trip, and Sally, my faithful, fourteen-year old Ford Escape traveling companion, was nearing the end of her life. I'd felt it even before we'd set out on the trip, but I'd decided to take my chances. I'd pleaded with her to stay with me the entire trip and told her that if we made it through together, I'd let her rest well when we returned home.

It wasn't a surprise when she started to shake, but what was a surprise was that the shake appeared to be coming from the steering wheel. I was pulling in to my destination in Phoenix, Arizona, and at first I chalked it up to bumps in the road. The next morning, my destination was California, but within minutes the shaking started up again, and I knew this was no bump in the road (except metaphorically). I pulled off and called around for a repair shop that could take a look that morning.

The shop that agreed to take a look at Sally seemed deserted, but after I pulled up, a petite woman with a curly cap of mousy brown hair came out from the back. After I gave her my keys, she told me it would be a few hours before they'd even be able to look at Sally and asked if there was anywhere I wanted to be dropped off in the meantime.

I looked at her hopelessly. "I'm not from around here, are there any parks nearby?"

She hesitated. "Well, there's one less than a mile from here."

"Sounds perfect."

She hesitated another moment like she was going to say something else but instead searched for the driver of the courtesy van. I wondered what that was about, but didn't ask.

This might have been a bump in the road, but only a small one. I'd budgeted in extra travel hours just in case something like this happened. So I called my Phoenix friend Katie and asked if she wanted to join me at the park. Despite being on the other side of town, she happily agreed to drive the forty-five minutes it would take to spend time with me. While I waited, I took the opportunity to explore the park by myself for a bit.

I strolled along the edge of pond stocked with fish, watching them bob up to the surface in hopes of their next meal. Turtles sunned themselves along the sloped, cement edge, plopping back into the water when I got too close. I waved to a few elderly fishermen propped up in folding chairs near a bridge traversing the water, small coolers by their sides. The landscape was all freshly manicured, much to the dismay of the ducks seeking their own nourishment. I couldn't understand why the woman back at the shop had any hesitation. This place seemed like paradise.

I slowed my pace when I saw it only took twenty minutes to walk around the pond. My second time around, I made a left onto the bridge. I was still wondering about the woman's hesitation at the shop and wondered if I was missing something obvious.

One of the fishermen had moved onto the bridge and was standing along the railing as another man was walking his bike toward me. I adjusted the strap of the canvas bag I'd had custom-made for this trip, pulling it in closer to my body. Then I exhaled and reminded myself that the majority of the people in this world were good, kind, loving humans.

I stopped next to the fisherman. "Have you caught anything yet?" I asked.

"Nah, but I couldn't ask for a better day," he said.

I nodded. At the same time, the young man on the bike was edging alongside me. I scooted closer to the fisherman while eyeing the young man on the bike skeptically. The hesitation of that woman in the office really had me on edge.

"One hug at a time? What's that?" he asked referring to the words I had printed on my bag for this trip.

"I'm on a cross-country trip building community one hug at a time," I replied.

The fisherman piped back up. "Oh! I love hugs!" he offered, opening himself up to the possibility of receiving one.

"Me too! I'd love one," said the man with the bike.

All the tension in my body relaxed, and I let out a soft sigh. My smile matched the brightness in their eyes. Without a word, I hugged each one of them, delighting in the magic of the day. I must have imagined the hesitation of the woman in the shop.

Just then my phone alerted me to a text. "Oh! That's my friend who's meeting me here. I've gotta go." I casually waved goodbye, finished my walk along the bridge, and made my way back to the parking lot.

Once Katie and I met up, we sat on stone benches a short distance away from the pond, where we heard loud cheering from a nearby pavilion. We turned toward the jubilant crowd, curious about what they were celebrating without balloons or decorations. When the cheering died down, we found ourselves distracted from our conversation by a five-year-old riding by on a toy unicorn, followed closely by her parents.

"What even is that? I didn't know they made toys like that. I'm jealous!" I said. Katie laughed in agreement.

Perhaps it was the sheer delight of the day that caused our final distraction to catch me so off guard. A slightly disheveled man who looked to be in his thirties sauntered over to me and Katie. He sat on a bench to my right and struck up stilted conversation. I felt unsettled, different than I'd felt on the bridge with the other two men I'd met that day. I wanted to honor the part of me that was uncomfortable, but I felt conflicted. Wouldn't it be rude and hurtful to exclude him from our conversation? What kind of message would that send when I was on a mission to build global community?

Katie and I entertained his awkward questions. I shared a guarded version of the trip I was on in hopes that I wouldn't need to give him a hug. No such luck. And there was no way I could say no to that hug, right? I mean, right? So I stood up and gave him a quick hug, holding my arms stiff and keeping some distance between us.

He took the opportunity to sit on the bench beside me. "You've got a great smile. I love your teeth," he leered at me.

I shifted uncomfortably and as imperceptibly as possible away from him.

He flipped a coin to Katie, who caught it, then turned back to me. "It's good to feel good, right? I mean, who wouldn't want to feel good? I think we should all have the right to feel good."

Confused, I just nodded my head, smiled politely, and said, "Yeah, we do."

He looked at me again, leaned in, and said close to my ear, "You really do have a great smile. Those teeth turn me on."

I froze.

Thankfully he was loud enough that Katie overheard. "Okay, that's enough. It's time for you to go," she demanded.

I looked to her like a child looks at a parent, grateful for their protection. Even though he wasn't close enough to touch me, I felt his refusal to move.

"Go. Now," she demanded more forcefully.

I felt his slow rise and snuck a peek as he walked away. He began swinging his arms and mumbling under his breath. When he was halfway across the park, my shoulders dropped, and I rose to give Katie a big hug. "Thank you. I appreciate you doing that."

"Do you know what that coin is?" she asked, holding the coin up in the palm of her hand. I shook my head. "It's a sobriety medallion. Twenty-four hours. I bet that's what was going on under the pavilion. Not sure when he was awarded this one, but it doesn't seem possible that it was today."

I knew what she meant. That man was not sober. I thought back to the woman's hesitation in the auto repair shop. Maybe she'd had a similar experience and wanted to warn me against it, but she'd learned, like me, not to be "so sensitive." I hadn't necessarily felt unsafe in that moment, but as time passed, I felt a pit growing heavier and heavier in my stomach.

After I got Sally back from the repair shop, still broken but with another appointment for the actual repair in San Francisco, I headed back out on the road to spend the next night with a multigenerational, multicultural family in Los Angeles. Amidst our deep conversations about racism and equality, I felt the pit in my stomach gain mass. I didn't think it had anything to do with the open, vulnerable conversations we were having.

I ignored it and remained as present to the family as I could. I must have done a decent job because the next morning before I left, the youngest family member, a five-year-old boy, presented me with a picture of a heart he drew just for me, asking if I would please come visit again. I leaned down and opened my arms, inviting him into what turned out to be one of my favorite embraces of the trip. I'd hoped it would soothe the pit still waiting for me, but as the hours passed, it continued to expand.

When I had stayed with my friend Margaret in Austin, she'd generously offered to coach me through any sticky moments during the trip. I thought back on the profound coaching I'd received from her in the past and tucked her offer away in a corner of my mind. Now, I texted her to ask if she had some time to help me debrief a situation. We scheduled a call for later that day while I was making the five-and-a-half-hour drive between Los Angeles and San Jose, California.

After explaining what had happened with the unsober man in Phoenix and how I was left with a growing pit in my stomach, Margaret said, "Melinda, he violated a boundary. He didn't have the right to say what he did or behave the way he did."

I heard the echoes of my stepdad's voice reverberating in my head when he said the same thing about Simon from the coffee shop. My mind started spinning. "What do you mean, he didn't have the right?" I asked. Logic said that I couldn't stop someone from doing what they wanted, so my brain was very confused by this statement. At the same time, my body felt clear. The Nudge was agreeing with her. I stared out at the dry landscape around me and the empty highway ahead.

"Everyone deserves to have their personal boundaries respected and upheld. He violated your personal space," she explained.

"But he wasn't even really that close to me, I wasn't afraid he would harm me," I countered, still not comprehending what she was telling me. Ironic, since respecting other people's boundaries has been one of my most important principles during MYOH.

"He made you uncomfortable. He knew he was making you uncomfortable and deliberately did it a second time. That was not okay," she replied.

Tears streamed down my face. I wondered how it had taken me over forty years to understand that I deserved personal boundaries just as much as anyone else.

Then the memories started flooding back. Memories of all the times I'd been told or shown that I had no control over others' actions. Memories of the way my few attempts at creating boundaries had been met with accusations of being too sensitive.

I realized I'd gotten pretty good at boundaries when it meant saying no to a task or event, but when it came to standing in front of another human who made me uncomfortable, I didn't know I had the right to say no. My sensitive self knew right away when my boundaries were violated, but my people-pleasing self spent so much time ignoring her and denying her needs that I'd forgotten she was the alert system I needed to listen to. People-pleasing was something recognized and reinforced by not just me but by most of the other girls I knew, and as far back as middle school. Ignoring boundaries was what we did.

I had dreaded computer class at Rochambeau Middle School. On the days I had class, I made sure to wear a turtleneck. I even had the sleeveless kind I could wear in the warmer months. I'd wait and enter the class only after the last bell rang. I'd quickly make my way to a seat in front of an open computer and turn it on. While waiting for it to boot up, I'd scan the classroom, searching for the teacher and praying I'd be able to determine where he was without making eye contact.

On a good day, I was ignored and left completely alone while attempting to avoid death on the Oregon Trail, a game we were allowed to play endlessly during class. On a bad day, I was targeted. I'd feel a hand on my shoulder and hot breath on my neck. "Do you have any questions?" the teacher would ask as an excuse to hover over me and lean in close.

"No, thank you," I'd say, shrugging my shoulder to remove his unwanted hand from my body while disgust sent chills through me. Clearly, my body knew a violation had just occurred.

After class, the girls in my grade would congregate in the hall. On a day when I wasn't targeted, I'd hear, "Did you see the way he was looking at Jill today? Eww. He was hanging all over her."

"Yeah, she must have forgotten what day it was. Did you see how low her top was?"

"She probably made his day."

We were all sensitive enough to know it was wrong, but none of us did anything about it in the moment. Only eleven and twelve years old, we already knew we'd be called too sensitive. We'd already become people-pleasers. We'd already forgotten that the disgusted chills running through our body were part of an alert system meant to compel us to create a boundary. We already knew our boundaries meant nothing.

Chapter Six

I didn't view my negative experiences with people as cause to stop loving or believing in humanity. On the contrary, I sought to better understand, to find reason to have deep compassion for those who seemed to deserve it the least. I embarked on MYOH to prove that all humans are loving and kind, worthy of care and concern. I wanted desperately to be right.

Most of the time, the people I hugged that year welcomed me with open arms. They laughed and told me how much my hug meant to them even when we didn't know each other. Sometimes people nearby would overhear, and I'd find myself in a group hug among strangers.

There were moments that took my breath away. One day during MYOH, I stopped at the country gas station less than a mile from my house. It had only one pump and looked perpetually deserted. I'd never used it, not even for last-minute convenience items. In fact, when I ran out of gas while mowing my lawn, this station didn't even cross my mind. I tossed an empty gas can into the back of my car, left the kids with Chris, and prepared to drive to the nearest QT gas station ten minutes away.

I almost missed what was right in front of my face. At the stop sign at the top of my road, I could only make a right or left because the gas station was straight ahead. Muscle memory prepared me to turn right, but at the last second my brain cleared of whatever distracting thought it was chewing over, and I saw the gas station. "Duh," I said out loud.

I giggled at myself, turned off my blinker, and drove straight into the gas station. I inserted my bank card and waited for the prompts on a screen that looked older than me. Nothing. Ugh. I debated moving on and going to the QT anyway, but I couldn't justify driving ten minutes further just because I couldn't use my card at the pump.

Inside there was a woman behind the counter who appeared to be in her mid-fifties. The protective plexiglass barrier she stood behind, long before Covid, had two large openings right next to each cash register for transactions. She turned from stocking cigarettes. "How can I help you?"

"I just need a couple gallons of gas, and the card machine out at the pump isn't working."

"Oh, yeah, that's been out a while. I can get you over here." She pointed to the machine closest to the door.

After she finished ringing me up, I debated just turning around and walking out without asking for a hug. The barrier had a large opening, but was it large enough for two people to hug through? Besides, I probably smelled after being out in the hot sun for an hour mowing the grass.

Something compelled me though. "This might sound funny, but can I give you a hug?" I asked.

Her head whipped up to look at me, eyes wide with disbelief. "Yes, yes!" she exclaimed, walking briskly out from behind the counter to join me face to face. We wrapped our arms around each other, and she leaned in to close any gaps between us. I felt the desperation in her embrace and maintained the hug until she was ready to let go.

After moving back from the hug, she continued to hold on to my arms and looked directly in my eyes. "An angel has sent you to me, I know it. My mom just died last week, and I know she sent you. I really needed that," she shared with tears in her eyes.

My eyes welled up as she leaned in for one more quick hug. "Thank you," she whispered into my ear. She let go of me, looked into my face one last time, then returned to the counter.

I wordlessly backed out the door, in awe of the invisible forces at play that orchestrated that moment.

It wasn't just the people I hugged who left me breathless. About a month after I began MYOH, I searched for communities of other bloggers who might support and inspire me as I wrote about MYOH each evening in my own blog. I quickly found myself making friends in these communities. We'd read each other's posts, share experiences, and build friendships across the web.

One of these friendships was with Shabana. She lived across the globe in the small island country of Bahrain. We'd offer each other virtual hugs and encourage each other's journeys. She'd mentioned the difficulties of hugging in her culture, but it wasn't until I read a guest post she shared on my blog that I understood the magnitude of my privilege here in the United States. I am free to hug.

Of all the freedoms I'm blessed with, this is one I take most for granted.

I Hug More. Because of a Blogger on the Other Side of the World

My name is Shabana. I live in Bahrain. It's a small is-land nation in the Arabian Gulf. It's a Muslim country, and societal norms dictate men and women shaking hands a taboo, let alone hugging each other. (The high school I went to has a rule that boys and girls, boys and boys, and girls and girls are forbidden to shake hands longer than 30 seconds. No, I'm not kidding.) So obviously, the majority of the people here don't hug (unless there's been a huge calamity or someone in the family died.) Women do the traditional air-kiss (muah-muah on either side of the cheeks, in case you didn't know) when they meet but hugging as a greeting? No way! And here I was, a closet hugger. I looooove hugs. I come from a family where my mom hugged us three children a lot. But the sad truth is, it stopped there. Hugs from Mom. That's it.

Which is why I thought that what Melinda was doing was so brave. I met Melinda at an online blog-ging forum. I was intrigued by the name of her blog—myyearofhugs.com—and clicked on it. I was truly amazed to see that this lady was on a mission to hug as many people as she could every day, and document those hugs as well as her day, every single day, on her blog. I mean, I felt awkward hugging my friends and family, and here's this lady who asks complete strang-ers for hugs! I loved it!

I read her blog regularly and all the little life lessons she was learning along the way. And I really, really wanted to do something similar. (My wildest aspirations included putting up a booth giving free hugs, but thoughts of the government locking me up for being so "open" killed those ideas quite quickly.) I knew I had to start small. So I started hugging my family more. And friends. And soon enough, they caught on. I'm happy to say that now when friends meet me (men included), we hug, as opposed to a dry, business-like handshake, which is the norm. My younger brother hugs me quite often now, which is really saying something, as he's the shyest in the family. I even send out lots of online hugs (and get many in return!). I'm trying to hug more and more people every day, and it feels fantastic! And all this is thanks to Melinda!

How could I not believe in humanity with experiences like that? I felt the desire for love and connection was at the heart of every human.

Most people would agree—to a point. "Sure," they'd say, "but there are exceptions. There are truly evil people in this world. Just look at how full our jails are."

My response was usually not well-received. "What if no one is truly evil, only not well-loved?" I'd say. "Circumstances can cause people to do things very out of character."

"So you don't think there should be punishment?" they'd ask.

What? My eyes would squint as I tried to process how they went from hearing me offer compassion for humans to assuming I didn't think there should be consequences. I'd shake my head and defend myself. "Of course there should be consequences. I just think that if we offered a little more compassion and understanding to people, there'd be less need for those consequences."

"Yeah, but rules help keep people in line, and if those rules are broken, then they have to pay the price," they'd nonsensically counter.

"I don't agree. I believe that if humans maintained their heart connection and were left to their own devices without rules, they'd naturally desire to do the right thing. I believe we're wired that way, which is why it feels so bad when we hurt someone unintentionally."

This was almost always met with something like: "You live in a dream world, Melinda. Your utopian society could never exist."

I'd leave these conversations feeling frustrated because I didn't have the words or time to explain what I meant.

I knew that the utopian ideal I was describing wasn't possible in the world we were currently living in. What I didn't get to explain was that I knew if we dropped all the rules tomorrow, chaos absolutely would ensue. More people than ever would do the wrong thing because there'd be no threat of punishment, confirming their point. But I also didn't get to explain that I believed it was the rules creating some of the pain that caused people to lash out to begin with. I didn't get to explain that it was societal expectations and fear of abandonment that caused humans to misalign from their hearts in the first place. I didn't get to share that I believed the utopian ideal would only be possible if we were willing to let things get chaotic at first. If we were willing to accept the mass confusion and panic that would come from this newfound freedom, and choose instead to let the rules go a bit at a time, in baby steps. It would take great courage and strength to be willing to walk that path, but if we dared, I believed that the utopian ideal would be waiting for us on the other side.

Beliefs, however, can be shaken to their core.

Chapter Seven

"How do you explain wars, Melinda?"

I got asked this a lot during MYOH. As if wars automatically proved that humans were evil, as if it were that simple. I'd answer that the decision to choose war or violence was based in fear—fear of losing control, fear of powerlessness, even fear of rejection. That explanation soothed the fear inside my own brain. I needed to believe in humanity's capacity for love and kindness.

Then on a crisp, clear December day in 2012, just months after I completed MYOH, my entire belief system was shattered.

". . . reports of children killed by an intruder at an elementary school . . ."

These were the first words I heard the moment I turned on the radio as I drove to pick up Cooper from his elementary school. Even though the DJ announcing the news didn't pause, my mind was flashing so fast I had enough time to think, "Please don't say in Connecticut," as if I already knew that's where it was.

". . . in Sandy Hook, Connecticut," he continued.

Chills ran through my body in an explosion of adrenaline. My mind held a thousand questions while somehow also going completely blank. Thankfully, Parker was sleeping soundly in the back of the car. My head swiveled back and forth as I desperately searched for a place to pull over. I couldn't drive and manage the emotions going through me at the same time.

The radio became background noise, continuing to fill me in with the very limited details they had. I knew someone who might have more information. I prayed she could tell me it was a mistake.

Mom worked at *The Newtown Bee*, a local paper in Newtown, Connecticut, the town that housed the smaller community of Sandy Hook. It also bordered Southbury, my own hometown. I took dance lessons at the Newtown Town Hall for fifteen years. I visited my great-grandmother at her quaint home in Sandy Hook until she'd passed twelve years earlier at the age of eighty-six. One of my good friends, who had elementary school-aged children, lived in Sandy Hook. I needed more information.

"Newtown Bee, this is Sue, how can I help you?" My mom sounded so calm.

"WHAT'S HAPPENING?" I screamed at her, wondering how she could sound so normal.

"What do you mean?" she asked.

What did I mean? What did she mean, what did I mean? She had to know what was happening. She was at the freaking newspaper. "They're saying there's been a shooting at the school? Is it true? Is it true!?" I continued to scream. I couldn't control myself. Thankfully, Parker continued to sleep.

"We don't know what's happening yet," she replied, remaining unnaturally calm. "No one has gotten any confirmations. A few reporters are at the scene, and hopefully we'll have more information soon." So she did know. How was she remaining so level-headed?

"Lori's kids might go to school there, Mom. They might be there," I cried.

"Honey, honey, I know. Calm down. There's nothing you or anyone can do right now. We just have to pray and hope for the best," she said, trying to soothe her panicky daughter.

The realization hit me then: it was true. This was really happening. And there was nothing I could do about it. I began sobbing, my breath coming out in hitches. I was able to stop only when I feared I might pass out.

Parker often took his longest naps while in the car, so I always left about an hour early for Cooper's pickup, using the extra time in the carpool lane to meditate or read. After getting off the phone with my mom, I raced to the school, unable to wait one second longer than necessary to have Cooper in the car with me, safe where he belonged. The carpool line was already around the block. Apparently I wasn't the only one desperate to see their child.

I composed myself to the best of my ability over the next few days around the boys, especially once I knew Lori's kids were safe, but I was a mess anytime I had a moment to myself. The truth was so much worse than I could have imagined.

School shootings were increasingly on the rise in the years leading up to 2012, but never in my wildest imagination could I have predicted they'd be possible in an elementary school. I raged along with the rest of the country—until someone would mention the evil of the shooter. Those conversations scrambled my brain. They went against everything I believed in humanity. I didn't think evil was possible, but how could there be any other explanation for something so incomprehensible as opening fire on young children?

Despite my confusion, when others mourned the twenty-six people lost, I unpopularly mourned twenty-eight. Some understood and agreed that the shooter's mother deserved to be mourned along with the children, bringing their count to twenty-seven, while others felt she was just as guilty for raising such a monster. But no one felt the shooter deserved to be mourned. I was alone in that grief.

Most of my belief in the goodness of humanity was extinguished with the first news report of that tragedy. But there was a flicker, a small flame, that refused to go out. A flame that imperceptibly grew over the next few years while I waded through the soul-sucking mud of confusion. I knew I needed to find a way to continue to grieve him along with his mom, the teachers, and the children who died that day. The Nudge told me so.

Most of the country believed he didn't deserve to be mourned. This belief "othered" him into something inhuman. To deny his humanity was understandable, but it also opened up the possibility that it was okay to deny other people's humanity as well. I knew I couldn't allow that to happen, even if I was the only one who continued to mourn him.

But I still needed to reckon with myself. What did I truly believe? How was this possible? How could I justify it? How could I explain to others that I even wanted to justify it? There was determination in the flame burning inside me, a patient resoluteness that waited for me to return to the truth it held.

Calling someone evil is taking the easy way out. It gives us a pass from having to look at our own capacity for harm. It creates a separation that allows us to other another human being. This road is a slippery slope. If we can so easily other someone we've determined to be evil, what constitutes evil? Is it murdering someone? What about self-defense? Is it only when one murders children? Here I began to see just how slippery that slope was. My mind drifted back to a time I tried to forget.

I was fifteen at the time, and I was in the car with my dad. As he drove, I stared down at my hands and noticed I was wringing them.

Dad must have noticed too. "How are you doing?" he asked.

I lifted my head and turned it slightly to face him as he peered over at me from the driver's seat. I gave him a smile that didn't reach my eyes.

"I want you to just breathe with me," he said. "Take a deep breath in and out slowly through your nose."

I let him lead the pace as we breathed together mindfully.

"In through the nose, out through the nose," he repeated. "This slow breath has always helped to calm me down in stressful situations. Just keep breathing every time you start to get nervous again. Breathe in through your nose and now out through your nose."

We continued to breathe together until we pulled up to the doctor's office that had delivered the news of my pregnancy just weeks before. It had been less than three months since I'd lost my virginity. I didn't get pregnant that first time. I knew better. I always insisted on using protection. But subsequently, when the condom my boyfriend and I were using broke, I didn't need a test to tell me the outcome. I already knew I had an impossible decision ahead of me.

I spent weeks thinking about it. I couldn't have a baby. I was too young. I had too many aspirations. I didn't want to get married, even though my boyfriend was willing. Selfishly, I couldn't imagine having to deal with the judgment that would follow me down the halls of my high school as my belly grew and became undeniable. I couldn't burden my parents with caring for an infant when they were still raising their own babies. I was too young.

I was certain I was doing the right thing.

At the clinic, I lay on the cold table and stared up at a ceiling with images tacked up from a comic strip whose main character was named Melinda. Unsure if that was meant to be a sign or not, I took comfort in these images while my stomach cramped and I ignored the truth of what was happening.

When the procedure was over, my dad held my arm to support me out to the car. "How are you doing now?" he asked.

"I want lunch at Ponderosa," I answered with a youthful smile spreading across my face. I was unaware of just how lucky I was to live in a time and place where abortion was legal and I didn't have to wade through a line of picketers at Planned Parenthood.

"Well, I take you wanting to eat as a good sign." He smiled back without judgment.

I knew the abortion was the right decision for me at that time and while I continued to reckon with the myriad of feelings that come with making a decision like that, I stood by it.

It would have been easy for me to other the Sandy Hook shooter in the belief that there was a difference between what he did and what I did. And that's more than valid. But also, blankly othering him would have kept me from knowing the depth of a human soul. It would have kept me from acknowledging that I was not so different from him. It would have kept me from allowing my heart to be broken into a thousand pieces by the tragedies of human existence. Tragedies that were so complex and vast that to reduce them to one label would cage not only the person we were labeling but ourselves as well.

Allowing myself to open up to the possibility that I might not have understood why he chose to shoot elementary school children but that I could understand he was a complicated human just like myself expanded my capacity for love in ways I didn't even know were possible.

I realized that it was less about finding an explanation for someone's behaviors and more about allowing for the possibility that they were as infallible as me. I realized that if I allowed myself to other another human being, it meant I was an other too.

* * *

It took time to process the depth of the confusion and heartbreak I felt following the stark contrast between MYOH and the Sandy Hook shooting. I had no idea how to do that, so I just kept going through the motions of life, numb to it all. I was afraid if I allowed myself to feel, I'd drown in despair.

By the time I came across an advertisement for nature-based coach training, I was desperate. I needed to find sturdy land I could rest on. I signed up, and in those first few months of training, I slowly found some footing. This was despite the fact that my family had just relocated from Raleigh, North Carolina, to Atlanta, Georgia, leaving behind the only life preservers I'd had: my friends and church community.

Training to be a nature-based coach reminded me of who I was as a child—running barefoot through the woods, collecting magic stones in the creek, and talking to fairies. It reminded me of the beauty I saw in all of life. It reminded me that there was even beauty in the fallibility of humans. Near the end of the training, I was invited to an in-person retreat in New York where I'd get to meet all of the people I'd spent months cultivating relationships with online.

The retreat temporarily allowed me to fully engage in life again. I communed with others around a campfire and joyfully played Capture the Flag under cover of night. In this spirit of play and imagination, I connected back to myself and shook my head clear of the demands culture placed on me. I returned to my wild and tasted a freedom that was ripped from me at a young age when it was implied that I wasn't enough.

The last night before the retreat ended, we were invited to watch an optional video not included in the curriculum. I declined. Instead I found a soft spot in the grass under the stars where, splayed out on my back, I wept over the disconnection between the future the retreat held out as possible and the one I was returning to. I wept for a world I wanted but didn't know how to get—one that embraced all of humanity.

Finally, long after the others went to bed, I reluctantly returned to my room and fell asleep, knowing that no matter how much I delayed the inevitable, the world that was not as I wanted it to be demanded my return.

The next morning, I walked downstairs as the first light of the sun entered the kitchen. Everyone else remained asleep in their beds. In the warm comfort of the historic home where we were staying, I was grateful for the modern convenience of the coffee maker. I needed a jolt of caffeine after the limited, fitful sleep I got. In no rush to advance the day, I carefully poured non-dairy creamer in my coffee and stirred in a spoonful of sugar. Then, holding the coffee in one hand, I grabbed my journal and Bic pen in the other and headed outside past the place where I'd been lying in sorrow the night before.

The morning was brightening quickly and while there was a chill in the air, I was grateful no dew had formed on the picnic table I walked toward. I sat for a few moments, appreciating the quiet before journaling. Once I opened my notebook, I just stared at the blank page.

How do you write about a feeling you don't understand—or maybe aren't willing to understand? I didn't want to return home, but I desperately wanted to see my boys. I didn't know what I wanted to do with my life, but I knew things couldn't remain the same. I didn't know what I believed anymore, but I still needed to find something to believe in. Tears began flowing again, although not as fiercely as they'd come the night before.

This retreat was where I met Margaret, who would coach me on my cross-country hug journey years hence. That morning, she was beside me before I realized she'd even come outside. She sat with me in silence, waiting for me to be ready to talk. After a long five minutes, I raised my head and looked into her kind eyes. I raced through all the thoughts I wasn't sure how to write. All of my confusion and all of my fears. "I feel so lost. I'm not sure what to do or what's even real," I said, my head hanging low again as I summed up my confusion to the best of my ability.

"You know," she said, "'I don't know' is a complete answer."

I quickly raised my head and stared at her, dumbfounded, my tears drying up in an instant. I felt both clearer and more confused than ever. Of course I knew that "I don't know" was a complete answer, but the way she said it, or maybe the timing of when she said it, felt like the greatest epiphany I'd ever had.

After a brief moment of reprieve, the tears returned, and I didn't try to stop them. I felt foolish, childish even, that such a simple, obvious statement would cause me such grief, but Margaret simply sat there and held my hand until the tears subsided. She then wrapped me in a warm, motherly embrace—the kind that puts all the broken pieces back together again. More words were likely exchanged, but they were irrelevant. I'd received everything I needed in that one phrase: "'I don't know' is a complete answer." She sensed that I'd need a few more moments to process this simple, life-changing moment and left me to return to the rest of the group that was slowly waking up.

My brain recalled moments in my life when "I don't know" wasn't accepted as a complete answer.

As a junior in high school: "What college are you going to go to?" people asked.

"I don't know," I'd answer.

"What do you mean you don't know? You're running out of time to figure it out! What are you going to go to school for?" they'd ask.

"I don't know," I'd answer.

"Well, I guess that's okay. Some people aren't sure when they first go," they'd reply.

"No, I don't know if I'm going to college," I'd say.

"What do you mean you don't know if you're going? Of course you're going. What kind of future will you have without a degree?" they'd ask.

"I don't know," I'd answer as they shook their heads and made it clear that I was screwed.

In the early nineties: "Isn't it awful what's happening in the Gulf?" people would ask.

"Yeah, war is terrible," I'd answer.

"What do you mean? Don't you think it's necessary?" they'd say.

"Oh, I don't know. I guess I just don't know enough about it," I'd say.

"What do you mean you don't know? Don't you read the news? Don't you want to stay informed?" they'd press, insisting it was my duty to know.

I really tried to stay informed, but I didn't know what to believe. Conflicting reports were everywhere, and as soon as I thought I had the right answer, someone else was arguing with me about how uninformed I still was. It seemed I couldn't know enough to know the right answer.

But if I were honest with myself, I'd been pretending to know what people were talking about much earlier than that. It felt like I'd done it all my life.

In sixth grade, our lockers were directly in front of our classroom. After lunch, we'd congregate in front of them, waiting for our teacher to let us back into class. I tended to keep my head down and smile politely at anyone who looked my way.

As I stood there one day with my books in my arms, an outspoken, pushy girl from class approached me with a few others following her. "Hey Melinda," she sneered, "Are you a virgin?"

At eleven years old, I wasn't sure what that meant, but I couldn't let her know. So I confidently answered, "No, I'm a Leo."

Laughter erupted around me, and I knew I'd answered wrong. I willed my face not to turn bright red, but there was no stopping my shame from becoming evident. It wasn't the first time I'd been made to feel stupid for not knowing, but rather than embrace "I don't know," I doubled down and learned as much as I could about as many things as I could so I'd never have to not know again. An impossible goal.

In fact, even after the life-altering coaching moment with Margaret, I was still a long way from being able to say "I don't know" when someone asked something as deeply provoking as the question: "How can you have any compassion for someone as evil as the Sandy Hook shooter?"

I started to think I was defective as a human. The people around me continued to seem to have it all figured out. I wanted to know what they knew and how they knew it. What was I missing? What was wrong with me? Was I missing an essential part of my brain that held knowledge? Was I made wrong? Did God make a mistake with me?

It never occurred to me that the very people who were judging me for not knowing things already knew the answers to the question they were asking and may have been looking to validate or elevate their own status in some way. It also never occurred to me that some people asked questions simply because they were curious to get to know me better. I wouldn't have known how to differentiate the two anyway. Not that it would have mattered. I imagine it's really difficult to get to know someone who doesn't know themselves.

Chapter Eight

There was a foolproof way to be invulnerable, and that was to be perfect. I spent a lot of years trying to discover how to be just that—so agreeable, so likable, and so available that no one could ever say anything bad about me. It meant everyone had to like me, a goal I'd heard was impossible, but I was determined to reach it.

MYOH was a great way to do this. Who could possibly have anything bad to say about someone giving out hugs every day for a year? And it seemed to be working. People loved my journey. They loved me.

Near the end of MYOH in 2012, my story was picked up by *HooplaHa*, an "only good news" website. They wanted to interview me about my hugs. Their lead reporter lived in Connecticut, so it seemed like a great excuse to visit my family. I agreed to do the interview there.

"So how does this work?" the reporter, Steve, asked. "Do you just walk up to people and hug them?"

I was on edge as I stood in front of the local Shop-Rite. I naively thought he'd just want to talk to me, not that he'd expect me to hug people on camera.

"No." I watched the cameraman getting set up out-side the entrance to the grocery store. "I always ask for a hug first so I'm not just hugging some unsuspecting stranger. That'd be creepy," I laughed.

Reporter Steve laughed too. "Yeah, I wasn't sure. I did think that was kind of weird. Okay, so let's spend about twenty to thirty minutes here with you hugging people, then we'll head back to your mom's house to do the rest of the interview."

I nodded in agreement, but my nerves ramped up. I had spent more than 365 days asking people for hugs, but every time felt like the first time. My knees shook, my voice quivered, and the butterflies in my belly took to flight.

Now I was being asked to do it while being recorded. What if I got a no on camera? What if I ran into some-body I didn't get along with? What if it looked completely fake? Still, I did what I always did. I swallowed hard, took a deep breath, and plunged in. "Can I give you a hug?" I asked the first customer who passed by that day.

I didn't get any refusals that day, but something felt off. I had moments where I felt in the flow but mostly, there was an unpleasant quality to these hugs that hadn't been there before. Judging by the smiles on the reporter's and cameraman's faces, it was imperceptible to them.

After twenty minutes had passed, Steve told me he had enough footage. I let out a sigh and walked over to where he stood next to the cameraman, Mike, who was still filming.

"Melinda, that was incredible. I don't know what I'd been expecting, but it wasn't that," Steve said, his eyes filled with wonder.

I asked what he meant.

"Just the outpouring of joy and, well, not to be trite, but love I just witnessed. People trust you. You brighten their day. Just watching, you've brightened mine," Steve added while Mike nodded in agreement.

My face colored with a combination of pride and . . . shame. I didn't know where that shame was coming from, but I suspected it had something to do with why I was feeling off. I plastered a smile on my face as wide as it'd been on my wedding day to prove I was just as joyful as I thought they expected me to be.

"I want to ask you one last thing on camera before we head back to your mom's for the rest of the interview," Steve said.

Once I agreed, Mike trained the camera on my face while Steve asked the question that helped me piece together why I felt so off: "So Melinda, now that your Year of Hugs is over, do you think you'll continue to hug people?"

With the wide, wedding smile still plastered on my face, I answered, "Are you kidding? I love hugs. I couldn't imagine ever wanting to stop."

This was absolutely true and also a big, fat lie. I did love hugs. I didn't want to imagine stopping. Only I could imagine it, and I'd imagined it every day since the journey was over. I was tired. So damn tired.

As soon as I answered that last question, the shame that colored my face when Steve was complimenting me overtook any pride I felt. "Fraud," it said. "Liar. Disgusting."

I accepted its judgment. I was a disgusting liar. I had tricked people into believing that this hug journey was the greatest thing that had ever happened to me. I'd fooled them into believing that all I cared about was sharing love with others.

Shame relentlessly continued to dog me, bombarding me with questions I didn't know the answers to. "If the only reason you were hugging others was to share love, then why did you feel so ashamed?" it hissed. "Why did you want to stop?" Then, after a beat, the most important question of all: "Why did it excite you so much to be the one in the spotlight?"

I figured shame knew the truth. I was a fraud, only doing this for the glory. I didn't deserve to be interviewed. I didn't deserve the recognition; it was just freaking hugs after all. People did this every day. What made me so special?

When I returned home from my Connecticut visit, I forgot about the interview and returned to everyday life. I slowly tapered off the number of strangers I hugged each day. I encouraged my blog readers to share their own hug stories, so I could take the spotlight off myself for a while. I got a few people to post, but mostly I was on my own. My blog numbers started dwindling until Steve's story was posted on *HooplaHa*'s site.

"Melinda, Melinda, wake up." Chris spoke gently, knowing I was a light sleeper. "You're going to want to see this." He knew that the only time I'd expect him waking me at two in the morning was if something was wrong and he didn't want to scare me.

"Huh? What?" I answered groggily.

"Come take a look," he said.

My frustration spilled over into anger. I felt like I was still trying to catch up on the sleep I'd missed in the first years of my kids' lives. I gauged his energy, determined it wasn't an emergency, and demanded it wait until morning.

"No, you're not going to want to wait. Your story's been picked up by *The Huffington Post*."

My eyes shot open while my brain was still attempting to process the news. "What?"

Chris tugged on the blankets and encouraged me to get up again.

I stared at the ceiling while my mind buffered. After a brief moment, I yanked the covers off and followed Chris into our media room, where his laptop was set up on a tray table connected to the reclining chairs where he sat every night.

He sat down and turned the computer to face me. Sure enough, there was my story front and center on *The Huffington Post*. One of the reporters had seen the video posted on *HooplaHa* and wrote their own article about it. In a few short hours, it had received enough interest to be a top story.

I wanted to pump my fists and jump up and down in celebration, but I was still so damn tired. "Babe. That's amazing," I said with as much energy as I could muster.

"Let's bust out the Veuve and celebrate with champagne!" he said.

As much as I wanted to celebrate in that moment, I reluctantly asked to delay the celebration until the following night and surprised myself by actually going back to bed.

In the morning, I rolled over and found Chris still wasn't in bed. It'd been a long time since he'd pulled an overnighter for work, and I always worried about him when he did. I didn't hear the kids stirring, so I went to check on Chris. I found him sleeping soundly in the leather chair where I'd left him the night before. Tiptoeing away, I went downstairs to enjoy my coffee in the peace and quiet.

The coffee was nearly finished brewing before I remembered. My story. It was a top story on *The Huffington Post*. The amazement and excitement I'd felt just a few short hours before wanted to burst forth with squeals of delight, but I didn't want to wake Chris or the boys. Instead I did a quiet, happy dance before pouring my coffee and grabbing my iPad off the kitchen counter where it was charging.

I sat at the kitchen table, the soft light of dawn offering an ethereal quality to everything it touched. I barely noticed. I wanted to open my email and discover what messages awaited me, yet I also wanted time to expand so I could make the moment last. The anticipation was so sweet, I wanted to savor it. I took a moment to look out the wall of windows to my left while I willed my right leg to stop bouncing.

I took a deep breath, forcing myself into the present moment. I watched a house finch lift off our birdfeeder just as a chickadee came to feast. I listened to the hoot of the mourning doves I'd once mistaken for owls. I lifted the steaming mug of coffee to my lips, taking my first sip. Placing the mug back on the table, I paused for another brief, anticipatory moment, then slowly lifted the soft blue cover protecting my iPad. I was ready to discover what amazingness others had to say about my journey now that it was rendered so public.

My inbox was filled with messages from all over the world:

> *Hi Melinda!*
>
> *I am writing to tell you I loved your Hug Project! I was reading the news online this morning and I saw an article about you in our Brazilian news website. Very nice! I will follow your updates in your blog and hope you get lots of hugs every day! Maybe, one day, if ever I go to US, or you come to Brazil or Canada, I will give you a hug ... for now, I just send you my online hug!*
>
> *Congratulations on your "project" and wish you all the best!! =)*
>
> *Cheers!*
>
> *(Ms.) Aline Abe*

> *Melinda,*
>
> *You are such a sweetheart! I wanted to hug my computer screen. :) You are a true inspiration and I virtual hug you (many times) for bringing a smile to the face of others. I'm a very shy person, but a very good hugger. I'm going to do my best to carry your message forward to the people around me.*
>
> *Mike*
>
> *Rochester, NY*

> *Hey Melinda,*
>
> *I just saw the little clip about you hugging your way through life on the Huffington Post and I just wanna let you know that I think that this is so great! I think it's a brilliant idea and such a simple but power-ful way to share love and affection, especially toward*

strangers. As there is quite a big distance between us, I'm sending you a virtual hug!

Best regards,

Sebastian from Berlin, Germany

I came across the story of your year of hugs today and I must say that I feel it is nothing short of revolutionary. This was truly the best news story I have ever read. Without much detail I can tell you that my life has been uncommonly harsh and a hug saved and changed my life in a very literal way. It is comforting to know that there are people with your capacity and depth for compassion still left. I appreciate you and the boldness you have exhibited by using a simple act to encourage everyone who has experienced or heard about it. You made my day and we have never met. Keep it up, hugs are contagious. I'm sure you know that.

James

I wept with joy.

Within a week I had magazine and radio interviews lined up, with TV interviews pending. I was having my fifteen minutes of fame and loving every second of it. People wanted to know more about this girl who was hugging strangers, and in that moment I couldn't wait to share.

I expected the interviews would remain light-hearted and full of love. I mean, they knew that's what they were getting, right? Wrong. Drama sells. After the first few radio interviews, I began to doubt myself. I don't even remember what questions were asked that made me feel like such a fraud, but

I know that after each interview, I felt less and less like I'd done something good and more like I was begging for attention. And how could that not be true when the attention felt so good? The shame I felt after the interview in Connecticut reemerged.

Halfway through my roster of interviews, I received an email that stopped me in my tracks, the only one I never replied to. The subject line was: "What Is Your Motive? What Do You Hope to Accomplish?"

> *Dear Melinda,*
> *What shall it profit you, Melinda, if you gave 1001 hugs in a year or two but lack genuine relationships beyond the superficial?*
> *Rebecca S, A Born-Again Christian Woman*

My blood ran cold. She caught me. She knew I was a fraud and called me out. With each radio interview I did after that, I became more and more nervous. I didn't know what to say. I was afraid more people would catch on that I was a fraud, even though I didn't know what the deception was. I'd hang up after the phone interviews feeling mortified by my stammering and inability to produce cohesive sentences. The TV interviews failed to materialize, and I assumed it was because they'd heard the shitty radio interviews and decided I really was that fraud.

Why did Rebecca's words cut so deep?

I'd struggled my whole life to gain and maintain genuine relationships, but often they eluded me. These hugs were a way to feel connected to a humanity I didn't seem to be able to build a relationship with. I didn't know why. I didn't know what I was doing wrong, so I often did seek out superficial relationships to feel some semblance of belonging. I didn't think anyone saw through me in that way, but Rebecca did. She knew. She knew I didn't belong.

She also called me out on the ways I was profiting off these superficial relationships with fame, attention, even gifts that people sent me. I didn't deserve it. I didn't deserve any of it. All I did was hug people, something most people do every day. Did I deserve all this attention for it? It was wrong to bask in it all. I was wrong to take advantage of my simple acts of kindness and make them into something that benefited only me.

I was so ashamed, I couldn't talk to anyone about this, not even Chris. I moved about my days, finishing the remaining interviews in a fog and going through the motions while feeling completely disconnected from myself. I breathed a sigh of relief when they were over; the shame only returning when the final magazine article about MYOH was published in the holiday issue of *Reader's Digest* a few months later.

Chapter Nine

Five years and one move to Atlanta later, I was no longer hugging or blogging. I'd become so disconnected from myself, I'd stopped doing anything I loved. At that point I couldn't have even told you what I loved. I just knew I was miserable, so I did what I'd always done. I turned to books.

I had questions. Why am I the way I am? How can I create a better life? Why am I so miserable when everything is going just fine? Why can't I just be satisfied with the life I have? What can I do as a stay-at-home mom to feel fulfilled? What am I missing that other people seem to know?

Following the bread crumbs, I came upon a book by Glennon Doyle, *Love Warrior*. She wrote about doing a practice for twenty-four hours where she'd yell *shut up* in her head to any negative thoughts her brain said about her. I knew I had a few negative thoughts bullying me and I thought it'd be a fun way to call them out. I decided to try it for myself.

The following morning, I walked downstairs to the kitchen of the townhome we'd rented in Atlanta. *Love*

Warrior was sitting on the counter, and I remembered that I meant to spend the next twenty-four hours telling my bullying thoughts to shut up. A smile flitted across my face. I was ready to send those bully thoughts packing and I figured this would be a fun way to do it. I didn't plan on writing down any of the thoughts. I just wanted to tell them to shut up.

The kids, now nine and six, were still sleeping, and I had at least thirty minutes before I needed to get them up for school. I turned on the coffee maker Chris had prepared for me the night before, grabbed my mug that said, "No Peopleing Today," and opened the fridge to grab some creamer.

"Are you sure you want to use that creamer? It's dairy. Full of fat that could kill you," said the critical voice inside my head I immediately dubbed Judgmental Melinda Brain (JMB).

Shut up, shut up, shut up, I countered in my head. I smiled. That felt good. I couldn't wait to try it again.

I didn't have to wait long. "Why haven't you gotten the kids up yet? You're not giving them enough time to get ready. You know they need more time than this," JMB said.

Shut up, shut up, shut up, I thought again as I watched the kids amble downstairs, having woken up on their own. After I prompted them to head back upstairs to change, they returned fully clothed and bright-eyed.

"Eww, you're going to let them wear that to school? Don't you care about what they look like?" JMB struck again.

Shut up, shut up, shut up," I continued to say in my head.

"What kind of a lunch is that you packed for them? Basic. Barely has the nutrients their growing bodies need," JMB said.

Shut up, shut up, shut up.

"And that's what you're packing it in? They must be getting teased in school, and it's all your fault," JMB continued.

I wasn't finding this fun anymore. *Shut up, shut up, shut up.*

After the bus drove away: "Now that they've gone to school, what are you going to do with your day? With your life? With yourself? Are you just going to be lazy and sit around again watching TV?"

Shut up, shut up, shut up, I countered while walking back inside. I brought my coffee over to the dining room table where my iPad was waiting for me.

JMB was waiting for me too. "Oh, that's right, you're just going to waste away your day scrolling. You don't do anything productive. And what about your husband? Did you bother making him lunch? Do you ever do anything nice for him? All you do is complain. You don't appreciate him or anything in your life, do you?"

Shut up, shut up, shut up. I felt like I needed to compensate for all this judgment by being some kind of productive, so I got up to brush my teeth and get dressed.

"Oh, good for you. At least you're taking care of your hygiene. Kind of. When was the last time you showered? What about exercise? Stop making excuses and just go freaking do it. You're growing wider and flabbier by the minute."

Shut up, shut up, shut up. I brushed my teeth, then put on some jeans and a tank top.

"Do you really think that looks good on you?" JMB said.

Shut up, shut up, shut up, actually I do.

"Oh," JMB said, more judgmental than ever. "Well, do you actually think anyone else would think that looks good on you?"

Shut up, shut up, shut up. Shit. This was definitely worse than I expected.

Chris got up minutes before he needed to leave for work, just enough time to get ready and walk out the door. He didn't know I was experimenting with my thoughts this morning. To him, it was just another day. He gave me a quick kiss before heading downstairs to his car and leaving for the Bank of America building in midtown.

"Your husband doesn't even want to spend time with you. He leaves himself just enough time to get ready so he can avoid spending any more time with you than he needs to. I don't blame him. You're such a nag," JMB spat.

Shut up, shut up, shut up. The words felt like they were losing their meaning. By the time noon rolled around, I fell in a heap to the floor, sobbing uncontrollably.

Oh my god. I actually hate myself.

The thoughts had been relentless and downright mean. I hadn't gotten a break from them all morning. I was dumbfounded. I thought I had pretty healthy self-esteem, but it turned out, I'd been faking it. I'd been covering up the more sinister truth: the greatest bully in my life was me.

I blamed Rebecca for calling me out as a fraud in her email after MYOH was picked up by the *Huffington Post* to account for the terrible interviews I'd had. I blamed the move as the reason I had very few friends. I blamed my confusion over Sandy Hook as the reason I preferred to stay home alone every day in the comfort of my own space. In reality, I was simply terrified that others might hate me as much as I hated myself.

I didn't start out that way. I absolutely adored myself as a kid. I was certain I was the funniest, smartest kid around. When I entered kindergarten already knowing how to read, I didn't flaunt it, I simply embraced my greatness. So when I was asked to be the narrator of the play at the end of the year, I jumped at the chance. I read *Are You My Mother?* by P. D. Eastman while the other kids in class acted out the scenes. I was brilliant; I didn't make one mistake.

By first grade, things in my life had begun to shift. Up until that point, my best friend was the only friend I'd needed, so I hadn't tried to make others. When her family transferred her to a new school, I felt lost and alone.

Toward the beginning of the year, my first-grade teacher announced that we'd be performing *Cinderella* just before the holidays. My hand shot up to play the lead role once again. I'd get to be the beautiful princess! That had to win me friends.

The teacher gave me a stack of stapled papers with all of Cinderella's lines highlighted. I was practically jumping out of my seat with excitement as I thumbed through the pages. It wasn't long before I felt a tap on my shoulder. A classmate was looking at me expectantly. She glanced back to make sure the teacher wasn't looking and whispered, "You know, Cindy really wanted that part."

I turned around and looked in Cindy's direction. Just at that moment she looked up and gave me a sad smile. I felt terrible. I hadn't taken a moment to consider whether or not someone else wanted the role. I felt greedy and started to wonder if keeping the role would actually make the other kids like me less. As bad as I wanted it, I wanted friends more.

I raised my hand, and when the teacher called on me, I said, "I don't want to play Cinderella. I want Cindy to have the part. I don't think I can remember this many lines."

I looked over at Cindy, and her face brightened immediately. The teacher asked if I was sure, and I nodded while handing the script over to Cindy's friend, who passed it back to Cindy. By the time she got the stapled stack of papers, her friends had gathered around her, congratulating her in a way no one had me. Cindy peered back in my direction and gave me a big smile.

I was so conflicted. It felt like the right thing to do, and my heart felt joy seeing her smile, but I felt so sad.

It was one of the first moments of disappointing myself that I can remember. Those girls didn't befriend me because I'd sacrificed a coveted role for Cindy, but that didn't stop me from trying that tactic over and over throughout the years. I'd gotten so good at disappointing myself that it stopped becoming a choice and developed into a habit.

I felt like I was doing the right thing every time I disappointed myself for the sake of pleasing another. I thought that's how I could make friends. I thought that's how I'd get people to like me. I even eventually thought that's how I'd keep my marriage together. I became the easy-going one. I'd go wherever my friends wanted to go, do whatever they wanted me to do.

Toward the end of high school, I'd made a new best friend who I did everything with—she even lived with me for a time. She loved to party, stay out late, even shoplift. It was all thrilling to me. With her, I felt like I lived on the edge.

It also felt wrong. It wasn't who I was, but the moments in between the partying and the shoplifting were the most fun I'd had with anyone. In those in-between moments, I felt more like myself than I'd had since I'd lost my best friend just before first grade.

In the in-between moments, she was also the most generous person I'd ever known. When I was diagnosed with multiple sclerosis, she found out how much money the medication cost and organized an entire fundraiser for me, raising over $4000.

The fundraiser was held at a bar, and despite the fatigue I felt after enduring a round of steroids for my most recent attack, I showed up. I wore one of the few outfits I still felt remotely cute in since my entire body was bloated from the steroids. I had bags with deep, dark circles under my eyes, but the minute I walked into the bar and saw her face light up from across the room, I knew the misery I'd feel over the next week for staying out late would be worth it.

And so it went. Where she went, I followed. What she wanted to do, I'd find a way to make happen. How could I not want to be friends with someone so generous and thrilling? I was terrified that if I stopped following and asked to lead, we'd no longer be friends. It wasn't until Chris and I were married that our friendship finally fell apart, and as awful as it was, it was okay because at least I had Chris. I had someone new to follow.

I lost myself completely in others for the sake of fitting in, for the sake of not being abandoned, for the sake of feeling loved. I'd just forgotten that there was only one love that truly mattered, and that was my own.

Chapter Ten

When I was pregnant with Cooper, I worked part-time at a hair salon in Ridgefield, Connecticut. The women in the salon had been with me through the healing of my multiple sclerosis, several pregnancy losses, and the success of my pregnancy with Cooper. We were close, often going out together after work. When Chris and I made the decision to move to Raleigh, North Carolina, the ladies were excited for me but seemed sad to see me go.

Sharon joined me by the register as she often did between clients. "I hate that you're leaving. I'm really going to miss you."

"I'll miss you too," I said.

"We'll keep in touch though," she added.

"No, we won't," I said. "We'll say we will, but we won't."

Sharon looked mortified. I didn't understand her expression. I thought everyone knew it was a given that when someone moves away people say they'll keep in touch, but they don't. I was simply stating a fact.

"Yes, we will, Melinda. What are you talking about? Do you not want to stay in touch with me?" she asked with an expression I now know was hurt.

"Of course, it's just in my experience I've never had anyone continue to stay in touch with me after we no longer see each other every day," I said.

"Oh my god, that's so sad. Is that true?" she asked.

"Yeah, I mean, it's no big deal. It's just the way it is." I was confused by her reaction. I began to wonder if people really did care enough to stay in touch. But as expected, I eventually lost contact with nearly all of the women in the salon other than an occasional Happy Birthday message on Facebook. A seed had been planted though. Do people other than family actually care more than I think they do?

It was six months after the revelation that I hated myself when I traveled to New York for the in-person part of the nature-based coach training retreat. Days before, we'd received a release form that included a request for dietary restrictions.

My heart both seized and rejoiced. After twenty years of needing to be the one to initiate any discussion of accommodation, I was grateful for the request. It was proof that the world had indeed come a long way toward understanding that some people really needed to be careful about what they put in their body.

Still, the old stories I'd told myself about what a burden I was for needing accommodation lingered. At the time of the retreat, I ate dairy-free, gluten-free, and vegan, the strictest of any diet I'd been on. I didn't see how they'd be able to accommodate me when, as I imagined, most of the meals would be made in bulk for the entire group. Then an even more horrible thought surfaced. What if, for simplicity's sake, they made all the meals vegan, gluten- and dairy-free, and everyone had to eat that way? I wouldn't make any friends once they found out I was the reason why. At this point in my life, though, my health was more important than making friends, so I added my dietary restrictions anyway and hoped for the best.

Chris and the boys drove me down winding roads to the farmhouse where I'd be staying in Rye, New York, after we'd spent a week visiting family in Connecticut. From the passenger seat, I passed the time trying to catch a glimpse of deer in the woods until the first wave of nausea hit, reminding me that the only place I could focus my eyes was on the horizon ahead of me. The anxiety of arriving at an unknown place with people I'd never actually met compounded the car sickness and left me weak upon arrival.

I squeezed my boys goodbye and gave Chris a quick peck. "You probably won't be able to reach me most of the weekend, but if there's an emergency, I'll text you the number to the farmhouse," I told him before we hugged goodbye. I wasn't sure if this was true, but I didn't really want to be disturbed.

I searched for Lynn or Michael Trotta, the husband-and-wife duo who were leading the training. I wanted to check in quickly so I could bring my bags to my room and get settled. Following the signs, I walked directly into the main room of the farmhouse, an oversized, open-concept dining room with a kitchen to my right. I exchanged pleasantries with a few of my fellow students, then made my way to Lynn.

"Hi, Melinda! It's so nice to meet you in person." Her sweet voice had a singsong quality to it that warmed me instantly. "You can sign in here. And Jenny, our chef, is taking care of all your food needs."

Chef? They had a chef feeding us this weekend? I was intrigued and optimistic. The nausea settled, and I felt strength returning to my body. More people began filing into the dining room, so once I confirmed that Lynn had everything she needed from me, I excused myself and followed her directions to the upstairs bedroom I'd be staying in with four other roommates.

Only one bed had been claimed, so my options were still pretty open. I walked across the perfectly kept hardwoods that looked like the original flooring from the early 1900s. I chose a bed along the wall opposite the door, tucked away in a dark corner of the room.

After a few moments of journaling on my bed while more students came and went, I felt replenished enough to join everyone mingling in the dining room. My timing was impeccable. Shortly after getting there, Lynn and Michael held their first meeting of the weekend.

It was during this meeting we were introduced to Jenny, the chef. She was a good friend of the Trottas and had been hired to prepare the meals all weekend. She was one of those people who seemed to have joy written all over her face, even when she wasn't smiling.

When the meeting was over, Lynn personally introduced me to Jenny. "Melinda," Jenny said, "so nice to meet you! I've had fun experimenting with dishes within your dietary plan." I felt warm gratitude flood my body as the Nudge informed me she was trustworthy.

Dinner was served buffet-style. Each dish had a label noting whether the dish was gluten-free, dairy-free, and/or vegan. It turned out that though I might have had the most restrictions, I wasn't alone in them. I breathed a sigh of relief and joined everyone else in line to grab a plate of food. The smells surrounding us were divine.

After loading up my plate just like everyone else, I made my way to one of the tables that was beginning to fill up with people. Tuning out the conversation around me, I looked down at this perfectly normal-looking plate of food. I didn't see any meat, gluten, or dairy, but I'd also never seen food that looked and smelled this amazing without those ingredients. I couldn't wait to dive in.

Taking the first bite of quinoa, I sank deeper into my seat in awe of the delectable flavors dancing on my tastebuds. I didn't know how Jenny had created such deep, intense, rich flavors without meat or dairy, but I sure as hell didn't want to ask for fear she'd made a mistake and I wouldn't be allowed to take another bite. I nearly licked my plate clean, unable to focus on the conversation around me. The only thing captivating my attention the entire meal was the next forkful of food going into my mouth.

The next day, we were going to a nature reserve where we'd practice our lessons before enjoying a picnic lunch. Jenny provided another large spread to pack our bag lunch with. Each dish had the same style labels as the previous night, letting us know which ones had dietary restrictions. Without refrigeration available, it was a lot of sandwich fixings and salads.

I eyed the salad I intended to bring for my lunch. In a rare set of circumstances, I found myself at the back of the lunch line. As a big-time foodie, I pride myself on always being at the front of the line, but I must've been caught up in conversation. I wasn't worried. No one ever chooses the salad.

As I got closer and closer to the collection of food on the table, my stomach dropped. The salad was nearly gone. *Okay, that's okay. It's fine. I'm sure there are other foods I can grab*, I said in my mind to soothe the panic rising up from the pit of my belly. I reached the table and looked at the only items left: sandwiches full of gluten and meat.

I could scrape up about half a cup of salad, but I knew that wouldn't sustain me through a day in the woods. My eyes widened with anxiety and I felt the sting of unwanted tears. *How could this happen? Who takes salad for lunch? Don't people know there are others who may not be able to eat any of this other food? Where is their consideration?* I was in an anger-induced panic.

Mostly, though, I was terrified. What if I didn't get enough to eat and I passed out at the park? It'd been over twenty-five years since that had happened, but if it did, I'd be mortified. My mind was grasping for a solution by blaming others without ever considering that I could ask Lynn or Jenny for help. I've always wondered where logic goes in the grip of anxiety.

Lynn noticed my panic, placed a gentle hand on my shoulder, and led me away to a private corner near the kitchen. "What's happening, Melinda? Are you okay?"

I felt her concern land upon me like a soothing, weighted blanket, but I was determined not to make a fuss. "Oh, I'm okay. I'm just trying to determine what to bring for lunch because it looks like the salad is out." I barely got the sentence out of my mouth before I began weeping, giving away the lie I just told.

"Oh, sweetie. Is there nothing for you to pack?" she tenderly asked.

There was no point in pretending any longer. "The only thing I'd be able to eat is the salad, but apparently that's what everyone else wanted, too, and now there's not enough left," I said, feeling like a child pouting over what's not fair. I placed my hands over my face, ashamed by how immature I must have seemed to her.

She was unphased. "Oh, sweetheart. I'll go get Jenny. She'll whip up something just for you."

I quickly yanked my hands away from my face, "Oh no, she doesn't have to do that. I don't want you to go out of your way for me." I was determined not to be "difficult."

Lynn got very still and serious. She grabbed both of my hands in her own so I couldn't hide my face and looked right into my eyes. "You are worth going out of the way for. We want to do this for you. Let us do this for you."

Her eyes drew me in, and I saw she meant every word. The surprising part was that I believed her. I believed that she truly cared and wanted to prove to me just how worthy I was in her eyes.

She gave me a long hug that patched those broken, unworthy pieces inside, unknowingly setting me up for a taste of what it might feel like so I could recognize it again in the future. I let her hug me for as long as possible until she needed to let go and tend to the rest of the group. But before returning to them, she found Jenny and asked her to prepare me a special lunch. Rather than appearing burdened, Jenny seemed excited by the prospect and quickly got to work.

That was the first time I believed it might be possible that someone could find me worthy enough that they'd go out of their way for me. It wasn't because no one had done it before, but because no one had ever done it without expressing how much extra work it would require of them.

And so when the time came that the Nudge implored me to take a cross-country trip building global community one hug at a time, I was curious about genuine relationships in the wild. What did care look like? What were people willing to do for one another? How did people who loved each other treat one another? Did it look like what I had in my relationships or did it more closely resemble something I thought was only available in the fantasy landscape of my imagination?

Was I worthy, somehow, after all?

Chapter Eleven

On the first day of my cross-country trip, my body was on auto-pilot as I cruised down I-285 toward my friend Amanda's house. From a distance I heard Ed Sheeran singing "Beautiful People" and realized it was coming from the speakers, so I reached over and turned up the radio. I let the music slowly permeate my soul until all that was left was the thrum of the tires, a sweet melody, and infinite possibilities ahead.

An hour later, I pulled up to Amanda's house. I'd been torn about starting so close to home. It seemed pretty anticlimactic to drive an hour away for the first overnight. On the other hand, it felt like the gentle chime of a bell, letting me know I'd begun.

The first thing I noticed when I walked through Amanda's door were the balloons decorating the living room. I tried to remember if she'd mentioned anything about her teenage son's birthday on Facebook. More decorations filled the kitchen, but before I could ask Amanda about them, she guided me toward the hors d'oeuvres she'd set out. "I got a whole bunch of different options hoping you'd be able to eat at least a few," she said.

My heart melted. By that time, I was eating dairy but was still gluten-free and vegetarian. It continued to surprise and delight me when people were willing to go out of their way like Lynn and Jenny did at the NY retreat.

When the doorbell rang, Amanda's wife, Lea, opened it to let three of their friends in. My very slow brain began waking up to what was actually happening. The balloons were for me. The celebration was for me. Speechless, I scanned the room again with fresh eyes. Did she really believe in me and this journey so much that she'd invited her close friends to kick off the trip with a celebration?

I got lightheaded and excused myself, telling Amanda I wanted to get settled in my room. There, in the privacy of my own temporary space, I took a deep breath as tears welled up in my eyes. The emotion behind the tears felt unfamiliar—or maybe so familiar I didn't want to acknowledge it. Looking back, I see that it was a deep feeling of unworthiness.

Who was I to be celebrated for an adventure that took me away from my family?

Why would her friends want to be a part of this celebration when they didn't even know me?

And, my recurring question: what made me so special?

In that moment, a switch flipped in me. A curiosity bubbled up, one that had me wondering how the other hosts might feed me if given complete freedom with no dietary restrictions. Between Amanda and Jenny at the nature-based retreat, I knew people were willing to go out of their way to accommodate my needs, but I didn't want that. I wanted the opportunity to eat whatever my hosts chose to feed me. I was nervous, but it was only a month. I could always go back to my limited diet when I got home if I started to feel sick.

After composing myself, I walked back into the living room and was bombarded with requests to hug someone named Elizabeth. She hadn't arrived yet, but Amanda and her friends made it clear I had to give her a hug. I suspected she wasn't a hugger, and I was right. When she arrived, I approached her and, honoring any boundaries she might have, asked, "Can I give you a hug?"

She looked at me with that familiar skeptical look I often got during MYOH. "Sure," she said while side-eyeing me. I leaned in, and we shared an easy, warm hug. The hug itself didn't have any tension nor did I notice any resistance to it. I wondered what the big deal was.

Eventually, we retreated to the fire pit on Amanda's pool deck to wind down the evening. I sat in the empty seat next to Elizabeth. The conversation ebbed and flowed while watching Amanda's playful dachshunds run in and out of the pool.

When the opportunity arose, Elizabeth leaned over and asked, "What was that hug about upstairs?"

I realized then that no one told her why I was there that evening. I explained my journey with MYOH and how I hoped to expand those hug connections through this cross-country trip.

She sat back in contemplation. "You know, I'm really not a hugger. I don't like to give hugs, but your story— man. I can see why you're doing it and I think it's a great thing. I think we need it right now more than ever. I don't know if I'll ever be converted into a hugger, but what you're doing? I can get behind that."

It was moments like this that reminded me the trip wasn't just about me. Amanda and her friends wanted to celebrate my journey because hugs matter. Connection matters. Love matters. I went to bed that night feeling filled by all those things.

I'd been posting on Facebook, looking for a host in the region between Alabama and Texas, and by the next morning, my posts were getting desperate. I had a host to stay with in Alabama that night and a host in Texas on the fourth night but nothing in between—and the distance made for more than the eight hours I wanted to drive between two cities.

My sister must have seen the anxiety in my posts because next thing I knew, she'd created a simple graphic. It had a map of the southeast and a big circle around the area I wanted to stay in with a request in bold letters: "HOST NEEDED IN THIS AREA." It was brilliant. I snatched it off her Facebook page and posted it on my own.

It was just the flashing light I needed to catch the attention of a middle school friend, Gigi. Less than twelve hours later, my third night was secured with her friend's mom in Metairie, Louisiana.

Stocked with a case of water for the trip from my host's home in Mobile, Alabama, I pulled up to a house in the deep south that reminded me of my grandparents' home in the northeast: a single-story brick ranch with a meticulously maintained yard. My host, Darla, ushered me in with a welcoming hug, then quickly excused herself to finish preparing dinner while I dropped off my belongings in the spare bedroom.

I spent a few moments journaling and acclimating to this new space, stopping when I heard a commotion coming from the living room. As soon as I stepped out of the bedroom, I found three new pairs of eyes staring back at me. Darla's daughter had arrived with her grand-daughters. After an awkward pause, they greeted me one by one with a hug.

Over the course of the evening, a few other family members arrived, and I was once again reminded of my grandparents' house. That's where we'd gather every Sunday for family dinner. This was turning into a Sunday family dinner even though it was only Saturday.

There were tables pushed together and chairs brought up from the depths of the house so that everyone had a seat. Incredible aromas wafted in from the kitchen as the girls excitedly told me about their latest endeavors. I asked Darla if I could help her cook, but she wouldn't hear of it.

When dinner was ready, I was invited to be first in line to fill my plate with all the goodness laid out in the kitchen. To my delight, it was exactly what I might expect from a homecooked meal in Louisiana. I loaded my plate with jalapeño cornbread, gumbo, jambalaya, and wilt-ed greens. Taking my plate back to the table, I slathered butter on my cornbread and waited for everyone to be seated.

After years of denying myself the pleasure of such rich foods, my mouth watered at the thought of that corn-bread, and I couldn't wait to take my first bite. After grace, I lifted it to my mouth, breathing in the aroma of sweet heat. I took a generous bite, and the cornbread crumbled in my mouth but not in my hand, a feat typically executed by someone who's spent years perfecting their recipe. And perfected it was. The heat from the jalapeños was exquisite, just the right complement to the sweet corn. I could have eaten an entire meal of just the cornbread, but there was so much more to enjoy.

While I was distracted by the pleasure of the foods in front of me, the conversation around me built in volume and drama, as it often does at the family table. The girls were eagerly vying for my attention, sharing their school accomplishments and, in the case of one of the preteens, a love of potatoes.

"You know, I'll be heading into Idaho on my trip," I said, connecting her favorite food to a state that was famous for them.

"Oh my god! You're so lucky! I love them so much! If I could find one big enough to live in, I would!" she exclaimed in the tone of playful absurdity common to young girls. It became apparent soon enough she was setting the tone for the rest of the gathering.

The stories continued around the table until someone brought up a particular uncle, and suddenly there was a palpable energy in anticipation of the story about to be shared. They all fought to tell it, but finally one of Darla's granddaughters took the lead. "This is a story of my uncle's poodle and a gator," she said with a giant smile. The laughter began when everyone noticed my confused face.

Dog versus gator seemed like a story destined for a tragic ending, yet the sly smirks and suppressed giggles around the table kept me guessing. I held my breath as I heard about this beloved poodle being yanked into the water by a gator while the uncle watched it happen, unable to rescue his dog in time.

My mouth dropped open as they described—each family member took turns sharing a part of the story—how the uncle ran back to the house to grab his shotgun, shot the gator, then sliced open its belly to retrieve his dog. I was disgusted and mortified, but the look on my face had the family in even greater hysterics. I couldn't help giggling despite my revulsion. Part of me still held out hope that the uncle was able to revive the dog, even though I could hear how crazy that sounded in my head.

Of course, that wasn't what happened, yet the family's laughter was still building. The rest of the story was told in short bursts by whoever was laughing the least at the time. It turned out the uncle was so distraught, he cleaned up and bathed his dead dog, then stored it in the freezer to be buried at a later point, I realized the laughter was hysteria from the absurdity of the tale and I was completely sucked in.

"Who bathes their dead dog after it was eaten by an alligator?" one of the family members asked through their laughter.

"Heck, who bothers to try to retrieve the dog in the first place?" someone else asked in between hitched breaths.

I couldn't help but match their hysteria. But my laughter didn't produce tears until the final question came from someone who already knew the answer: "So when did the dog get buried?" they managed to eke out.

"Never! I'm pretty sure it's still in his freezer." This breathless response resulted in the entire table losing their shit, me included. By this time, everyone had abandoned their food. We were laughing so hard we couldn't speak, much less eat. Hell, we could barely breathe.

When the laughter finally died down, we cleared the table, and hugs were given all around as the rest of the family dispersed and went back to their own homes. Darla and I spent a few more moments winding down together before I retreated to my room. On my bed lay a large box. Thinking someone dropped it there by mistake, I grabbed it, intending to return it to Darla. Then I noticed the top had handwriting, and it was addressed to me.

Surely I was mistaken. I'd already received so much. Opening the box, I found local items to remind me of my trip, including a Louisiana Starbucks mug. There was an abundance of snacks to keep me energized during my long road trips and a few other small gifts. I was at a loss for words. Tears of gratitude and overwhelm sprung to my eyes. I couldn't believe Darla had taken the time to put together such a thoughtful gift for me.

I thought about all that I'd received since I'd stepped foot inside this house. A New Orleans Saints T-shirt, this enormous goodie box, a stained-glass window Darla had made that was from her own personal collection, and the best gift of all, a seat at their family table. I was a perfect stranger to these people, and yet they'd welcomed me like one of their own. I softly cried myself to sleep that night, tears spilling out of my grateful heart.

Chapter Twelve

After hugs, meals were the second most important aspect for building connection on the trip. Because eating together creates a sense of physical safety in the body, it's a quick way to establish a foundation of trust. My hope was that sharing meals would facilitate deep, vulnerable conversations—and they did.

The meals each host shared were as diverse as the experiences I had with them. I naively thought I'd simply be an additional guest for dinner. I didn't expect that my hosts would use the meals as a way to celebrate me. And that wasn't the only unexpected development. The curiosity I felt about my hosts and their lives began slowly shifting inward. I wondered if I could be as surprised by myself as I was by the people I was meeting. I wondered if the stories I had told myself and so blindly believed could be changed.

When I arrived in San Antonio, Texas, I could feel droplets of sweat making their way down my lower back even as the air conditioner blasted my face. I was eager to get to Terry's house and into a more temperate environment. She was a gifted coach I'd met through Lynn and Michael Trottas' nature-based coach training in New York, where she'd made a far greater impact on me than I think she knew.

During the retreat, the Trottas illustrated the lessons they'd taught us over the previous six months. One day, they led us to a sturdy fallen tree, angled so that the highest point was about four feet off the ground. "We want you all to stand in a line on that tree," they directed us.

One after another, all eighteen of us lined up on the tree. The bravest of us had gone first and were standing at the point of the highest drop. "Okay," we then heard. "Now rearrange yourselves in order of age without leaving the tree."

We all looked at each another and then down at the trunk under our feet. We immediately bombarded the Trottas with questions: "How do we do that without falling? How do we know where we go? Do we line up from oldest to youngest or the other way around? What if we fall?"

Lynn and Michael refused to answer. We were on our own. Shyly, we each turned to the person closest to us and asked the normally forbidden question: "How old are you?"

Once I knew the ages of the people near me, I looked around to see how others were lining up. It looked like the youngest were being lined up closest to the ground, near where I stood. As one of the younger participants, I knew I was already in good position. So I remained in place while others cautiously grabbed onto me and inched their way past.

Once we were in order, we turned to Michael and Lynn for more direction. Michael was staring at the opposite end of the tree, where there was still some commotion. Terry was the oldest participant in the group and she wasn't yet in the right space. "What's going on over here?" Michael asked gently.

"I don't know how to get up there," Terry said. "My knees aren't in great shape, and I'm scared of falling."

"Have you asked the others around you for help?" Michael coached Terry.

"No, I haven't."

"How come?" he asked.

"I don't want to be the weak link. I'm already the oldest in the group and I don't want to hold everyone up and be the reason we fail this activity." She became teary.

"Ah," Michael said. "It's tough living in a world that doesn't honor our elders. A world that doesn't see the value they bring through wisdom and experience. It's tough feeling like age is the failure."

"Yeah," Terry acknowledged, letting her tears flow freely.

"How would it feel to know that the others around you right now want to help you?" he asked.

She shrugged.

He pressed on. "Can you let yourself be helped by them?"

"Yeah, but I'm still afraid of falling," Terry said. "I don't know that I want to be up that high."

"What's stopping you from telling them and asking them to go around you instead of the other way around?" Michael asked while we all watched the situation unfold.

"But then everyone else on the tree would have to move, too, and there's not enough room. They'd all have to squeeze in close together to fit," Terry continued to argue.

Michael nodded his head, communicating the validity of her argument while also coaching her fiercely with his silence.

Resigned, she turned to the two participants above her on the tree and admitted, "I'm afraid of falling. Can you both get around me so I don't have to move?"

The two participants happily obliged her, giving her hugs while using her for support as they shifted their body from one side of her to the other. The rest of us scooted down the tree as far as we could go to make room for everyone to fit in the condensed space. When we were all lined up again, this time in the correct order by age, we all cheered. When the celebration died down, we turned back to Michael to debrief the exercise.

"Terry, how do you feel?" he asked.

"I feel good, supported. It felt good to let others support me like that," she said.

"You deserve support," Michael reminded her. "You've given your all to this world. You've raised your children; you've made your mark on your family, friends, your community. It's your time to rest. Let all those that you've helped help you. You continue to provide so much value in your willingness to receive, in the wisdom you've accumulated through the years. In the act of allowing yourself to receive here today, you've given permission to all the younger participants here to see the value in growing old. You are now the elder. What a gift."

Terry sat down on the tree, put her head in her hands, and cried healing tears. We all wept with her, grateful to witness this moment.

I was also crying in gratitude at having witnessed a different future than the one I had known. I cried over the possibility that I might not have to grow old and become an automatic burden to the people around me. I cried over the possibility that I could not only still hold value when I'm in my sixties, seventies, eighties—I might just have more value. I cried over the possibility that others might feel grateful for the opportunity to care for me. It was a profound moment.

Now, stepping through Terry's front door, I felt gratitude to be able to share space with her once again. I also felt guilty. Wasn't I the one who was supposed to be doing more for her than she was for me?

After greeting me with a hug, she hobbled back to her chair to sit down. "I'm so sorry, I need to sit down. I finally got the knee surgery I needed, and it's taking longer than expected to heal."

"Oh my goodness, no need to apologize! I'm just so grateful to see you again!" I replied.

She then pointed to the room directly behind me. "That's your room for tonight if you want to put your stuff down."

I looked behind me and jumped at my reflection in the full-body mirror set back between two doors.

"Yours is on the left."

After dropping off my bags, I joined Terry in the living room, and we caught up for about an hour until her daughter Alexa showed up. I helped Alexa take the bags of food she'd brought into the kitchen and offered to help her with dinner. Like every other request I made to help with meals, this one was declined, but I insisted on at least setting the table.

"We're so excited to have you here, Melinda. This table is brand new, and we can't think of a better way to christen it than sharing dinner with you," Terry said.

The pristine, dark oak table was set in an alcove adjacent to the front door. The runner down the center matched the leaves falling outside. I sat facing the window, and Terry sat across from me. Alexa began bringing in dishes of food until a feast lay between us and then she sat beside her mother. We offered up gratitude for the meal, the table connecting us, and the time we had to share together.

I felt honored to be a part of this ritual as they shared how important the dinner table was to them to create lasting memories. Then they told me about Terry's ex, who was Alexa's dad. He had died less than a week before.

I was stunned into silence. I had no idea. Outwardly, they showed no signs of the grief I knew they must feel. I couldn't imagine losing my dad or an ex-husband and then entertaining someone I barely knew less than a week later. I struggled with receiving all their blessings. I wondered why I was included in such an important ritual at such a tender time. I felt even more guilty than when I first arrived and worried that I'd imposed on them, even though they seemed thrilled that I was there. Still, I refused to let the negative stories I carried about myself ruin the evening. Instead I did what I knew how to do best. I listened. I got curious.

I asked questions about Alexa's dad. I invited them to share more stories about their family and Alexa's job at a correctional facility. I held space for their joy while feeling awe at how they were able to hold that joy so compassionately for themselves. I wondered once again what was so special about me that they'd want to share this auspicious moment with. I mean, I knew why others were special and could celebrate their differences but for some reason I was blind to my own unique qualities. This time though, instead of coming from a place of shame, it seemed to come from a place of curiosity.

* * *

Drew continued the tradition of hosts going above and beyond for me as a guest in their home. I can see now that it's likely how they'd treat any guest in their home, but I had a story stuck in my head during the cross-country trip that I was more of a burden to be tolerated rather than a guest to be celebrated. It was part of the larger story of unworthiness that was, unbeknownst to me, unfolding as my hug journeys continued.

Drew pulled me into her home with a warm, strong embrace that reminded me of the strength of my Italian great-grandmother's hugs. My great-nana spent her days mostly confined to her rocking chair, but that didn't hinder her from pulling each of her great-grandkids to her chest and smothering us with her love. No matter how hard we struggled, she didn't let go until she was good and ready. In Drew's hug, I felt my great-grandmother's presence as strong as ever.

Drew and I had met at a weekend retreat where we'd learned how to hold sacred ceremonies. Maybe that was why, from the moment I walked into her house, I felt held in the energy of an unspoken ritual. She introduced me to her husband and cats, and then invited me to sit on the couch while her husband, Fred, brought my luggage upstairs to the room where I'd be staying. After I sat, she pulled out a large keepsake book that covered both of our laps. Fred joined us after dropping off my bags and sat in a chair to her right.

Both Drew and Fred were archaeologists, and in the keepsake book they'd captured moments from different sites they'd worked on. Their stories invited me into their world, one filled with adventure, wonder, and intrigue. Perhaps it was just a vocation to them, but to me, it seemed magical.

Over the course of the evening, we learned more about each other. I was surprised to learn this was Drew's second marriage. She and Fred had such an ease with each other. Maybe that should've been the giveaway. Nearly all the married people I knew were still on their first, and often they held so much contempt for each other I thought that was just how marriages were.

I'm sure we had dinner at some point that evening, but I don't remember any of the details. That meal has long since been overshadowed by my memory of the next morning's breakfast. I awoke to the delicious aroma of coffee and, eager for a taste, dressed quickly and left the rest of my belongings to pack later.

As soon as I walked downstairs, Drew asked if I wanted coffee. When I eagerly affirmed that I did, she very formally said, "This bean comes from Brazil. It's a special blend I order online. Please have a seat." She pointed to the chair at the head of the table. She was giving off fine-dining establishment vibes.

Directly in front of me was a sliding glass door to their patio. It was surprisingly lush outside for the mid-October day. The skies were clear, and I could see mountains in the distance.

Drew placed an elegant cup of coffee in front of me along with matching containers of sugar and creamer. I considered the etiquette for coffee. Was it like British tea, where you weren't supposed to clink the spoon against the cup? I took my chances and let the spoon do what it was going to do, knowing Drew wasn't the kind of person who would judge me either way. As soon as I was done adding cream and sugar to my coffee, Drew was back with a fancy glass dish of yogurt. Alongside it she placed a bowl of the freshest berries I'd seen outside of picking them directly from the vine.

"Oh my gosh, Drew! This looks amazing, thank you!" I said.

But she wasn't done. She placed a puffy, rectangular croissant in front of me, explaining that she'd baked it that morning using Ghirardelli chocolate. The steam rose, carrying with it the decadent aroma of fresh yeasty goodness combined with a hint of the chocolate tucked inside.

My mouth dropped open. "You made this this morning for me?" I asked incredulously. Her smile widened with pride, and she nodded. Predictably, I felt unworthy of such an opulent send-off, but I savored each bite, memorizing every sensation with such precision that my mouth is salivating as I write this.

If a camera could capture flavors and textures, the resulting photograph would be a framed masterpiece on my wall. The overnight unspoken ceremony ended with a final hug from both Drew and Fred. Despite the feelings of unworthiness that continued to show up, when I left their home, something felt different inside me. I just didn't have the words for it yet.

* * *

Some of my hosts shared simple, basic dinners with me. Some took me out to eat. Some lovingly prepared their favorite meals; others ordered pizza. Many invited their loved ones to share the meal with us. A few kept it relatively intimate.

Even when I'd show up long after my hosts had eaten, great care was taken to ensure my belly was full before bed. Most of the food I ate was full of gluten, dairy, and meat—things I wouldn't have normally touched—but I enjoyed every bite. I remained certain, just as I had when starting my journey, that the amount of love and attention given to nourishing me would surround the food with enough protection that only the best nutrients of each meal would fill my body. I had no reason to believe this, but I felt its truth deeply enough that I never worried about what I ate.

It wasn't until I was three weeks into my journey that I came to recognize just how well my body felt. I spent nearly every day driving between six to eight hours. I slept at a different home every night. I ate whatever was placed in front of me. I had deep conversations and even joined my hosts for dancing or hiking when the opportunity presented itself. Yet, rather than feeling depleted, I felt buoyed by it all. Almost invincible.

Chapter Thirteen

I nervously introduced myself to Clarissa over the phone, ready to address her concerns about hosting me.

"I hope you understand," she said. "Elizabeth [who'd connected us] is a great friend of mine, and I trust her completely, but you must see how vulnerable it is to invite someone to stay in your home."

"Yes, absolutely," I agreed. "I know it takes great faith to invite a stranger into your home, and anything I can do to put your mind at ease, I will. I'll also understand if you prefer not to."

"I guess I'd just like to hear a little more about what you're doing and why," Clarissa said.

Determined to reassure her, I told her why I was driving cross-country, then filled her in on my original year of hugs and how that had informed the details of this trip.

"Oh my, that's pretty spectacular," she said. "I still feel hesitant, but you sound trustworthy, and I think I'd like to be included in this journey."

I understood where she was coming from. I was nervous about staying in strangers' homes, but I also recognized the risk my hosts were taking. I never took one moment for granted, especially because I didn't know what I was walking into. I didn't know what troubles might be going on in my hosts' lives or how much work it might have taken to prepare for my arrival. It was a lot even for those who knew me, let alone those who didn't.

At the beginning of October, just a week into my cross-country trip, I arrived at Joan's home in Albuquerque, New Mexico. Joan and my Aunt Susie had known each other practically their whole lives, having grown up together in Western New York. The only thing I knew about Joan was that she was a Buffalo Bills fan, so I knew if nothing else, we'd have that in common.

When I pulled into Joan's driveway, I smiled at the welcoming, inclusive flags lining the flower beds along the path to her door. One said, "In this house we believe: no human is illegal, women's rights are human rights, Black lives matter, climate change is real, love is love, kindness is everything." I felt comforted immediately. She was my kind of people.

I heard a dog announce my arrival. Joan opened the door, and I walked inside, appreciating the air conditioning after another hot, sticky drive in the southwestern corridor of the country. We waited for her small pup to calm before greeting each other with a hug.

My eyes drifted up to the décor on her walls. There were Bills posters, indigenous art, and pictures of animals everywhere. It was like being embraced by the whole house. I wanted to spend hours poring over all the details, but that's not what I was there for. I tore myself away and brought my luggage to the spare room.

"I got you a ticket for the Hot Air Balloon Fiesta tomorrow," Joan told me as I reemerged. "You're going to want to take a shuttle rather than drive, and I suggest you catch the shuttle as early as possible." She was a longtime volunteer at the event and knew I'd added an extra day in Albuquerque just so I could go.

Going to see the Albuquerque Hot Air Balloon Fiesta had been on my bucket list since I was a kid. One of my favorite childhood memories in Connecticut was of being woken up by the whooshing roar of a hot air balloon floating over my home just after the sun rose. Barely awake, I'd run outside in my pajamas and bare feet to catch a glimpse and—if I was lucky—wave at the people in the basket. This had only happened maybe once or twice a year when the conditions were right, and it had felt magical. The thought of hundreds of them in the air at once was almost more than I could bear.

"The first shuttle leaves at four, so you'll want to be there by three-thirty," Joan said. "The church where you'll catch the shuttle is five minutes down the road. You do have some warm clothes, right?"

"Yeah, I knew I'd be traveling through the northern states at the end of October, so I wanted to be prepared." I glanced down at my shirt, which still bore the unmistakable sweat marks from that day's drive.

"You'll probably be needing them tomorrow. I suggest wearing your winter coat, even. The temps can get into the thirties," Joan advised.

I didn't even know how that could be possible, but she had to know what she was talking about, right? I mean the worst that could happen was that I'd need to take some layers off. I'd rather do that than be stuck being cold. I shivered just at the mere thought of it. "Will you not be joining me?" I asked.

"I have obligations with the church I don't want to miss," she said. "I'll be going to the Fiesta later in the week. You go and enjoy. You'll have just enough time to come back for a nap before I get home. I figured we could go to the cultural center later in the day, then meet some friends of mine for dinner."

I agreed with her plan but felt conflicted. I knew I'd be more comfortable having someone with experience join me for the Fiesta and keep me company, but there was a certain excitement my introverted self felt in getting to experience it alone.

I had not yet adjusted to the Mountain Time Zone, so it was fairly easy for me to fall asleep by seven knowing I'd need to be up by three the next morning. As it was, anticipation woke me up fifteen minutes early. I turned off my alarm and got ready to check off the number one item on my bucket list.

I checked and re-checked that I had everything. Ticket? Check. Directions? Check. Phone? Check. Wonder and excitement? Check and check. I put a sweater on over the t-shirt and tank top I was already wearing, then grabbed my winter coat, hat, and gloves just in case.

As soon as I stepped outside, I put them all on. *Oh my god, she wasn't kidding*, I thought. Starting up my car, I noticed that the temperature was twenty-seven degrees. Definitely not what I was expecting in New Mexico in early October. I shivered while waiting for my car to warm up.

I was nervous pulling up to the church. How would I know where to park? Would it be obvious where to go? Was it possible to take the wrong bus? I wished I'd thought to ask Joan those questions. Turning in to the church parking lot, I noticed clear signs directing me and released my anxieties with a deep exhale. I quickly found my way to a long line of people already waiting for the first bus.

Normally I keep to myself in new and unusual situations—especially on public transport—but I couldn't contain my excitement. I met an amazing woman, Monique, who at eighty had been to nearly every Fiesta, including the very first one almost fifty years earlier. "I remember there were about a dozen balloons at that first Fiesta," she said. "There was one cardboard sign announcing the event that was held in a field thirty minutes from where it is now." Her youthful exuberance and jet-black hair belied her age. We became fast friends, and to this day have remained connected.

I showed my ticket at the gates and let my bag get searched before following the pulsing crowd into the Fiesta. My eyes wandered in the dark. A long chain of food and souvenir stands were slowly getting ready to open on my right.

Determined to find a prime seat, I ignored the deflated balloons on my left and briskly walked straight ahead. My nose burned from the cold, and I lifted my scarf to protect it—but not before the scent of coffee reminded me of the early hour and derailed my plans.

A line had formed in front of one of the food stands, and I veered in its direction. While waiting my turn, I smelled the aroma of coffee mingled with the scent of breakfast burritos. "Hi, yes, can I get a coffee with cream and sugar? Oh, and also an egg and sausage burrito?" my belly forced me to say.

I secured my bag on my shoulder before grabbing the coffee in my right hand and burrito in my left, then set out again to find that perfect seat. I followed the crowd until I noticed a few people spreading out blankets and lawn chairs on a small hill just ahead of me. I liked the idea of having the advantage of being above the balloons as they filled, so I headed in that direction.

Dodging people left and right until I got to the hill, I climbed the marked path and sat in front of the fence at the top, patting myself on the back for finding a spot that gave me a natural barrier on both sides. I placed my coffee gently beside my bag on the flattest surface I could find and took my gloves off to warm my hands around the enormous egg burrito.

All of a sudden, lights flickered across the field. Two or three balloons began to fill. An announcer spoke over the loudspeaker to explain that what we were seeing was the dawn patrol. They'd go up to check the conditions in the air and ensure safety for the event. Meanwhile, the lights allowed me to see more of the flurry below, where pilots were preparing their own balloons for ascension. For the next few hours, I watched in wonder as some balloons lit up with the flame from the burner, rose into the air, and came straight back down. More and more of the balloons began to fill up, remaining in place and awaiting their cue.

I could barely sit still. I took what felt like hundreds of selfies, even though it was still pretty dark out. I was just too fidgety. Eventually I stopped so I could put my gloves back on. Without the warmth of the burrito, my fingers were getting numb, and the coffee had gotten cold long before. Just then, a dog balloon with overalls lit up directly in front of me and began filling with air. The sun was brightening the sky, and I felt the growing anticipation of everyone on the hill. It was almost time.

The announcer declared the conditions acceptable for the mass ascension. I learned later that these were the clearest and best conditions for the Fiesta in years. More balloons quickly filled, and the first ones launched. Within minutes, at least twenty-five or more balloons were already in the air. My mouth hung open in awe.

The next thing I knew, an hour had passed and hundreds of balloons were filling the sky with different shapes, sizes, and characters. My research later told me that this feat was only possible due to a weather phenomenon that creates the "Albuquerque box," a weather-related container that keeps most of the balloons in one area.

By nearly eight, even though I hadn't seen all the balloons lift, I felt complete. My dream was fulfilled, and the bucket list item checked. The adrenaline and coffee were wearing off, and I was sleepy. With a satisfied heart, I picked up my bag, took a few more photos, and started my way down the hill toward the exit. By the time I approached the bus, my hat, scarf, and gloves were off.

I slept until 10:30, when I heard Joan return home from church. Wiping the drool off my cheek, the memory of the morning came flooding back, and I smiled softly to myself. Joan knocked on my door. "Hey," she quietly said, "I wanted to let you know I'm home. We can get going to the cultural center whenever you're ready."

Unsure how warm it'd gotten outside, I kept my tank top on, removed my t-shirt, and added the sweater. I doubted I'd need my winter coat anymore, but I brought it just in case. "I'm ready." I said.

Joan looked at me holding my coat and said, "You won't need that anymore."

I brought it out to the trunk of my car, leaving it for the colder states ahead, and jumped in the passenger seat of Joan's car. By the time we'd gotten to the Indian Pueblo Cultural Center, I'd removed my sweater and was already sweating in my tank top.

Joan and I split up to weave among the artists selling their wares around the edges of the courtyard. We found each other again just in time for a ceremony to begin. We sat in chairs arranged in a circle while an elder grabbed a microphone and prepared to lead us in a prayer circle. He began the prayer in gratitude, inviting everyone in the audience to stand and join together in a healing circle. A handful of indigenous people stood.

"Everyone. You're all invited into the circle," he said while a few more non-white people joined the circle. "Everyone means white people too. I invite you into this space, grateful for you just as much as anyone else who's here. My people believe in forgiveness and gratitude for all God's creatures."

Shame flooded my body. I'd only recently learned of the trauma inflicted on indigenous families when our country was founded. A time when their children were taken from them, sent off to a "boarding school" to erase their culture from their minds, and be indoctrinated in the ways of the colonialists. Many of those children died from disease and abuse. I felt sick to my stomach. My ancestors were, in one way or another, complicit in this practice.

I felt this elder's grace wash over me. I felt his willingness to forgive. My legs were pulled forward by the power of his invitation. Standing in the circle, tears streamed down my face while reckoning happened inside my body. I was doing no one any good by clinging to my shame and allowing it to become a badge of honor. I had to surrender to the vulnerability of the moment and allow myself to be forgiven.

I openly cried as the elder placed his hands over my head and shared the energy of his prayer with me. I marveled at the strength of humanity in an entire community forgiving another for their own genocide. I marveled at the strength of this elder to hold such profound, powerful space for forgiveness.

I knew big magic was happening for me, but my own relationship with forgiveness was so complicated I simply let the magic seep into my bones. That was enough— for now, anyway.

We met Joan's friends at a local Mexican restaurant for dinner. Mariachi music floated through the air, getting louder as we neared the front entrance. The short wait for our table gave me just enough time to greet her friends with a hug before being led through several overcrowded rooms. We weaved our way around waiters carrying multiple margaritas precariously balanced on their trays. Once we were safely seated, I focused my attention on the women I was seated with and not the overwhelming din of chatter and scraping plates.

"Okay ladies, I'd like to know, what's your greatest dream and what's your greatest accomplishment?" I asked these women, who were all at least twenty years older than me.

Ellie was the first to speak. "That's easy. My wife, Amy, is my greatest accomplishment. She's the dream I never even knew I had." She gazed lovingly into her wife's eyes, leaving us all speechless. I was in awe of the love expanding before me.

"That's the sweetest thing I've ever heard," I finally piped up, hearts filling my eyes like a ridiculous emoji.

"How the hell are any of us supposed to follow that?" Amy said, breaking the spell. Laughter expressed everyone's relief at Amy saying what they all were thinking. The conversation continued with ease throughout dinner. I was reluctant for the evening to end, but I had another long car ride the next day to Phoenix, Arizona. After such an eventful day, I needed sleep.

Before drifting off, I spent time journaling my experiences of the day. None of these women knew much about me. They didn't know I'd be accepting of who they chose to love. They didn't know I'd want to celebrate that love as much as they did. Yet they welcomed me in.

Joan literally invited me into her home, and they all invited me in to the most vulnerable details of their authentic, private lives. Was it because they recognized me as a safe person to share their lives with or was it that they felt comfortable to share who they were with anyone around? Could I ever get that comfortable?

Chapter Fourteen

These glimpses I was getting into the lives of others were beginning to expand my awareness of what was possible. I wanted a love like Ellie and Amy had. I wanted to be cared for the way I'd been at the retreat in New York and the way I continued to be on this trip.

On my way to Iowa, Sara, a friend I'd known for about a year, called to let me know she couldn't host me that evening but still wanted to spend the day with me at her orchard. I wasn't worried about not having a place to sleep because everything on the trip seemed to always work out. Sure enough, as soon as I got to the orchard, Sara excitedly told me, "My friend Abby is going to let you stay with her tonight. She's not very far from here, and I know you'll love her."

Abby lived in a quaint second-floor apartment of an old home. She greeted me with a warm hug as though we'd been friends forever, putting me instantly at ease. She grabbed my suitcase, led me to my room, and told me to join her in the kitchen when I was settled.

I looked around my room and felt like a celebrity. Abby had placed a letterboard on the dresser that said,

"Welcome Melinda" next to a tray filled with snacks. On the bed was a wicker basket with spa essentials: fuzzy pink slippers, a white robe, and travel-sized toiletries.

I didn't understand. Why would she go out of her way to do all this for me when I was staying with her for less than twelve hours? I glanced back at the letterboard. Melinda. *Yeah, that's me.* This really was all for me. From a perfect stranger who didn't know me at all. I was overwhelmed by the attention to detail she'd paid. It was hard to receive attention when I didn't feel I was doing anything for her. Or any of the hosts I was staying with.

I felt less like an honored guest and more like a freeloader who had nothing to give back. When I was deep in the shame like that, I forgot that my hugs and intentional presence were my way to give back. Not to mention the fact that I really wanted to believe that it was enough just to be who we are. It was easier for me to accept that in others than in myself.

I joined Abby in the kitchen and gave her another hug—a hug meant to convey gratitude but also love for someone I didn't know. She was willing to make a perfect stranger feel cared for in a way that said she didn't need to know me to understand our shared humanity. We stayed up late into the night talking, far past any acceptable bedtime for either one of us. In the morning, she sent me off with a protein-filled breakfast and promises to stay in touch.

* * *

Clarissa opened the door and welcomed me with a hesitant hug. We hadn't spoken again since that first conversation when she shared her concerns about hosting me, a stranger, in her home. She politely led me to the room where I'd be staying. I dropped off my luggage, then followed her for a tour of her home.

"Would you like to go see my backyard?" she asked. "I spend most of my time out there. We can even see if my husband's still working in his shed."

"Yeah, that sounds great," I said. "What does your husband do?" When she told me that he tumbled crystals as a hobby, my eyes widened. "Are you serious? I love crystals!" I said. I'd always wondered how the tumbling worked and how they got the rocks so smooth. I couldn't wait to find out.

When Clarissa opened the door to her backyard, I temporarily forgot about the crystals. She'd created a fairytale setting back there. Like, literally, I'm pretty sure fairies lived there. Greenery and flowers were everywhere, edging up to but not overcrowding the walkways that ran through the yard. I felt like I'd stepped into a real-life version of *The Secret Garden*.

As we walked toward the shed, Clarissa pointed out the different varieties of plants, offering up names I knew I'd instantly forget. In that space, everything felt so alive. I felt so alive. The shed peeked through the canopy. Rather than detract from the beauty of nature, it added to the magic of her garden.

Clarissa knocked on the door, peeked in, and asked her husband, Paul, if he was open to a visitor. He must've agreed because she opened the door wider for me to walk in. It looked like any generic workshop space with boxes piled up and tools hanging along the wall, but when I turned toward her husband, I noticed the crystal spheres lined up along his workbench.

I pointed to one. "Is that an ocean jasper?" I hadn't even said hi.

He rose from his swivel chair, picked up the sphere I'd indicated, and said with surprise in his voice, "Yes, actually, it is."

I rambled on about my love of crystals, especially spheres and ocean jasper.

"Huh," he said with a smile on his face, clearly reveling in the appreciation I had for the work he did. "Would you like to see how a sphere's made?"

"Are you kidding? Absolutely!" I said, unable to contain the wonder and excitement in my voice.

I'm not even sure at what point Clarissa left, but after an hour or so of my listening raptly, he finally said, "It's probably about time for dinner. Are you ready to head back to the house?" I wasn't, but my stomach was, so I reluctantly agreed.

Clarissa had already ordered some pizza and, after washing up, I joined them at their picnic-style kitchen table, where we happily ate and talked. "You know, Melinda, I'm really glad I agreed to host you," Clarissa said. "You are everything Elizabeth said you were and more. It's been a delight getting to know you."

My cheeks burned with pleasure.

Clarissa and Paul refused to allow me to help, so I remained sitting while they picked up. Somehow they got on the topic of a trip they'd taken and I listened as they reminisced.

"Do you remember that time in Paris?" Clarissa asked.

"Oh yes, that was our fifteenth anniversary, right?" Paul answered.

"Ahh yes, it was. Remember the song that played in that restaurant?"

He sighed in pleasure. "Oh yes, the restaurant with the rose trellis?"

"Yeah," she said, "that's the one."

The conversation continued, but it was obvious that I was witness to this walk down memory lane, not a participant. They gazed lovingly into each other's eyes as though more details of these memories could be found in them. They giggled like teenagers in love at their own inside jokes while continuing to clear the table. I was enraptured by this highly choreographed dance they'd clearly been practicing most of their lives together. Their affection was palpable. I held my breath for fear of breaking the spell they were under. They hadn't just built a fairytale with their garden, they lived and breathed it every day, and for one brief moment I got to play a background role in their enchanted story.

I'd been told for years fairytales weren't real. That a love like that wasn't real. How could I continue to believe that was true after this encounter? After seeing what Ellie and Amy had? Were they the exceptions to the rule or was it something available to everyone? Even me?

Chapter Fifteen

Connecting with people through hugs gave me the false sense that most of my interactions on my journey would be positive. I didn't expect it to be all sunshine and roses, but I didn't think there would be anything all that surprising. I was wrong.

I was driving across the west side of Texas, where everything was brown and flat, and listening to the audio book of Malcolm Gladwell's *Talking to Strangers* to pass the time. The only reason I stopped was to fill up Sally's tank after passing a sign that said, "Next stop for gas, 121 miles."

There was an eerie quality to this stretch of road, a loneliness that seemed to be emanating from the earth itself. I felt somber, so I turned the audio book off and passed the rest of the time in silence. As I neared my next destination, El Paso, I saw cars lining up in rows to stop at a booth. I hadn't expected tolls on this stretch of highway, but luckily I had a little cash on me. I opened my purse and began rummaging.

As I got closer, though, I realized it wasn't a tollbooth but a border patrol checkpoint. My heart grew heavy. I was aware of the thousands of children being separated from their parents under new policies enacted by Trump, and it made me sick to my stomach.

I watched as certain cars were singled out, the occupants forced to stand in the oppressive, dry heat while their car was turned inside out. I was repulsed when I realized before I even got there that my appearance ensured I wouldn't be one of those people. I didn't see how anyone within close proximity of this dehumanizing practice couldn't be affected, whether they agreed with it or not.

I didn't have enough time to shake off the feelings of sorrow and disgust before arriving at my friend Anika's home, but I plastered on my best smile, grabbed my luggage, and walked up to her front door.

Anika, like Drew, was someone I'd met at the retreat for sacred ceremony in upstate New York. In fact, she was my tent mate. When I'd arrived at the campgrounds for the retreat, snow was falling. I'd spun around in delight until I realized we'd be camping in that weather.

Having moved to the south more than ten years previously, I was no longer equipped for those temperatures. That first night, my zero-degree sleeping bag was put to the test, and it failed spectacularly. I was wearing three layers of clothes, five pairs of socks, a hat, gloves, and my big puffy jacket that covered my legs to below my knees. I still couldn't get warm.

After Anika arrived at the campsite, we set up the two-person tent, tucked our belongings away, and left to join the others. Despite the weather switching from snow to rain, the temperature remained pretty much the same. Luckily—or stupidly—our group was the only one in the entire park camping, so we took advantage of an unused campsite with a roof and stone fireplace to warm up that evening.

After we went back to the tent, Anika and I carried on a conversation late into the night. I tried to get some sleep, but it was nearly impossible. I had uncontrollable body shakes from the cold, rocks pressing against my back, and there were screams coming from nearby rutting elk that sounded like they were right outside the tent. When morning came, I had a newfound appreciation for all the modern comforts of home.

I didn't take those multiple layers of clothing off for the next three days. Yet despite my poor hygiene, Anika and I bonded. When she found out about my cross-country hug trip, she eagerly offered up her home as a place to stay.

After a quick hug, Anika ushered me inside. We passed the kitchen on our right as she led me to the dining room. "Supper's almost ready, and I'll lead you to your room when we're done. Maybe then we could go for a walk?" she asked, retreating back to the kitchen. From an open partition in the wall, I watched her get back to preparing dinner.

"That sounds great. I could use a walk after all that driving," I said. Something felt off, but I assumed it was the remnants of my sorrow from passing through the border control.

In that moment, Anika's husband walked in and sat at the head of the dining room table. His body language was closed off, so I remained seated rather than force the hug. "Welcome," he said in a friendly tone. "I hope you like spice. Anika makes excellent food."

As he sat down, Anika's two kids filed in from different parts of the home.

"Melinda, these are my children," Anika said from the kitchen. They each said a quick hello, seemingly uninterested in me. In fact, no one seemed interested in anyone else. There was silence as we waited for dinner.

I felt awkward. Did Anika tell them I'd be there? Was this just teenage indifference? Was I imagining a tension in the air? I was beginning to think that maybe border control wasn't the reason I was feeling off after all.

Anika served us dinner, neglecting to fill a plate for herself, and for the next several minutes all I heard was the clinking of silverware on plates and the soft sound of chewing. I looked around the table, but everyone's eyes were cast downward.

I asked the daughter, who appeared to be of high school age, how school was going.

"Fine." She didn't look up.

Before I had a chance to ask any other questions, both kids got up from the table, already finished with the meal I'd barely started. As soon as they cleared their places, Anika's husband got up, cleared his own place, and walked out.

I wondered if this was normal. I wondered if I'd done something wrong. Maybe it was tradition to remain quiet at the dinner table in Indian culture? I berated myself for not researching the culture before I got there. I turned to Anika, who'd just settled down to eat as the rest of her family got up. She smiled at me. "How was everything?" she asked.

"Delicious, Anika. Everything was wonderful," I said and smiled back.

"Are you ready to go for a walk?" Anika asked as soon as she was done eating and I was done clearing my place. When I nodded, she said, "I hope the rain holds off for us. If it does, the walk should be very pleasant. There's a park nearby. We can walk there and back."

"I'm sure it'll be wonderful even if it does rain. Anything beats that snowy, cold tent," I said, and we both laughed at the memory. I was anxious to connect with her away from her home and family. I wanted to know if it was just my imagination, part of her culture, or if I really was picking up on something amiss.

There was a slight drizzle as soon as we stepped outside, but it stopped before we even had time to get an umbrella. Once we'd left her property, I felt lighter, and our conversation flowed with greater ease. I shared elements of my journey with her and passed along greetings from friends we both knew. By the time we reached the park, people were coming out: parents pushing their kids in strollers, young children riding their bikes, older couples strolling hand in hand.

Anika guided me to the edge of the park, where we found a semi-dry patch of grass to sit on to continue our conversation. Over the next hour or so, we talked about the significant challenges in our marriages and wondered how to move through them.

"That was it," I thought. That was the tension I was feeling. It was so familiar I didn't recognize it right away. I was amazed that Anika had the strength and energy to host me in her home with all that was going on in her marriage. Maybe I was a good distraction?

Our conversation went deeper than any we'd had during the snowy camping trip. Perhaps that was because of the timing of what was happening in her life. Maybe it was the hugs. I'd seen that the physical act of hugging seemed to lower people's defenses and allow for greater vulnerability. The more vulnerable a person was, the more connected I felt to them.

*　*　*

I went to a relatively small high school. I didn't know everyone by name, but I certainly knew all their faces. When a school is that small, it doesn't take long for gossip to spread like a filthy germ, soiling the reputations of those talked about.

When I was a sophomore, I was accused of coveting my older cousin's boyfriend—who was also my own ex-boyfriend. My cousin and I knew we were family, but that was the extent of our relationship. Until the gossip started. The jeers that followed me down the hall came from multiple voices, but none of them were louder than my cousin Holly's.

"Slut." "Whore." "Stay away from David!" I had absolutely no interest in him anymore, but these voices belonged to seniors, my cousin among them, and I knew that to deny these attacks would only make them worse. I didn't know Holly that well, but slander coming from family still hurts.

All these years later, I was surprised to hear from Holly that she wanted to host me in San Francisco. But the years had softened my memory, so I thought maybe they'd done so to hers too. I saw this as an opportunity to move forward as a family. I was nervous but excited to lay everything out on the table and maybe even get an apology.

After foolishly taking my car with automatic steering that broke back in Phoenix down the "crookedest street in the world," Lombard Street, I pulled into the garage beneath Holly's building and shook out my aching arms. It had taken more strength than I'd expected to wrestle Sally down that road. I walked to the elevator and pushed the button for Holly's floor. When the elevator opened, I saw her door immediately. I took a deep breath to calm my nerves, stepped forward, and knocked.

Almost instantly, Holly opened the door, and with an enthusiasm that caught me off guard. She pulled me in with the kind of great big bear hug often reserved for people who've spent years missing each other. I was grateful but confused.

"I'm so happy to see you, Melinda! Come in, come in!" she exclaimed. "Do you remember Seth?" she asked gesturing to her husband. "He went to our high school, too, but it took years before we reconnected again and got married!" There was a vague familiarity about the guy but I can't say I remembered who he was.

"I'm so excited!" she continued. "We're going to go see the Blue Angels tomorrow—you said you still have time for that, right?" Before I could answer she went on. "Oh, and I hope you don't mind sleeping on the couch. We only have the one bedroom."

"No, of course I don't mind. I just appreciate you letting me stay," I said, curious how the rest of the visit would go and wondering when I'd get a chance to bring up the past.

That night, we gathered in her small kitchen. Seth was beside the refrigerator, chopping up fresh red peppers, while Holly and I prepped the rest of the salad. The

window was propped open, and Holly spotted me noticing it. "Isn't it great? This isn't like the East Coast. We
can just keep the windows open with no screens and not
worry about any bugs coming in."

"That's amazing," I responded, wondering if California was really all that expensive and calculating when I
could move there.

After supper, we retreated early to bed to rest up
for the long day ahead. I laid the sheets Holly had given
me over the couch, did my evening journaling, and wondered once again how I was going to talk about what had
happened in high school. She was so joyful and excited to
have me. Was she just trying to make up for the past? It
didn't feel like she was; her excitement felt genuine. I decided to just let the next day unfold and bring it up when
the time felt right.

The next morning, we got up early and packed a
cooler full of snacks and drinks to enjoy during the Blue
Angels Air Show. The timing and the synchronicities that
allowed me to experience such amazing events time and
time again on this trip was blowing my mind.

Once we were all packed, we left Sally in the garage
and piled into Seth's car. The trip to the Golden Gate
Bridge was short, and as soon as we parked, Seth guided
us to a green space with breathtaking views of the bridge.
We laid out a blanket, set up a few chairs, and relaxed
while we waited for the show to start.

For a city as large as San Francisco, Holly and Seth
seemed to know a lot of people. They introduced me each
time another friend of theirs passed looking for their own
place to sit. The hugs came easy, and with each embrace I
was woven into the cloth of Holly and Seth's community.

It was clear this wasn't going to be the time or place to bring up old pain. I was beginning to wonder if I even cared.

The first aircraft released into the sky were sky-writing planes, but instead of writing words, they flew straight up into the air, released their colored smoke, and then made daredevil drops and rolls back down, leaving red and blue plumes streaking in patterns in their wake. A few other planes graced the sky, but everyone held their collective breath when the Blue Angels finally made their debut.

The precision with which they flew together was mesmerizing and terrifying at the same time. I couldn't tear my eyes away, so when the formations broke and they flew in different directions, I wasn't sure which one to follow. I bounced back and forth between a couple until I couldn't see any of them anymore.

The next thing I knew, I felt heat rush over my face while my hair swirled about me. The sound of the engines was deafening, and the vibrations set off more than a few car alarms. I looked up just in time to see the last of the red-hot engines tear across the sky directly overhead. I stopped breathing. I remembered to start again when the five planes met up to fly under the bridge together in formation.

There was so much laughter, excitement, and wonder that day that by the time I left Holly's place, I'd forgotten all about our past.

Was it possible that simply through one's ability to change, hurt could be forgiven without expressed consent? I wasn't sure. All I knew was that because of the changes Holly had made over her lifetime, forgiveness came easy and wordlessly. I wondered if the magic of the blessing by the elder at the Indian Pueblo Cultural Center had anything to do with it.

Past disagreements were one thing, but current disagreement another. While in Phoenix, I found it challenging to remain open and vulnerable when I met up with someone whose viewpoint turned out to be far different from my own.

I had the opportunity to go to dinner with a friend I'd met through our mutual love of dogs and books. Samantha and I had spoken on the phone a few times, and I was excited to meet her in person. We actually had so much in common that I falsely—or naively—believed we had everything in common.

I pulled up to the restaurant where we'd agreed to meet and instantly wondered if I was wearing an appropriate outfit. The columns framing the front entrance felt more formal than any outfits I'd brought with me—not that I had many to choose from. My entire travel wardrobe consisted of only four outfits: two for warm weather and two for cold.

With no other option, I walked in with a sweater draped over my arm in case I needed to hide the well-worn tank top I'd chosen as one of my two summer tops. The hostess led me to a table tucked in a corner of the restaurant. After greeting Samantha with a hug, I pulled out the chair facing her and sat with my back to the rest of the room. I felt exposed.

"How's your next book coming along?" I asked her after we placed our orders for dinner. She was working on her third novel in a spiritual romance series that had me hooked. While she didn't divulge any major secrets from the new book, I listened with rapt attention just in case she slipped.

I'm not sure how the subject of the upcoming divisive election came up. It wasn't a topic I typically led with in any conversation. I just remember that after the first lull in our conversation, I felt blindsided.

"I'm just so grateful for all that President Trump is doing for our country," I heard Samantha say as my focus narrowed on her face. Was she being serious? She said something about the economy, but as I held my breath and tried to focus on her words, everything started sounding fuzzy. I felt the urge to counter everything she was saying, but I held my tongue. This trip wasn't about politics, it was about making connections.

My mind reminded me of lessons I'd learned from Brené Brown. In order to shift from debate and into connection, I needed to really hear what she was saying and believe her because her perspective was valid.

I began to sweat. I once again reminded myself that she was being vulnerable, sharing her truth on a topic that's fraught with tension. To keep the connection going, I needed to remain present and not run away from the table screaming like my body really wanted to do. My head began to ache from the tension in my jaw.

I didn't say anything as she continued praising the man who'd authorized ripping children from their families at the border. I felt like a traitor nodding at what she was saying, even though my efforts were only to make her feel heard and not like I actually agreed with her viewpoint. But the physical sensation of nodding felt like agreement and turned my stomach sour.

It took a few minutes for me to recognize the somatic signs I was experiencing. But once I did, I marveled at the way trauma gets stored in our bodies, reemerging as a warning signal whether the threat is real or imagined. My body was reacting to the powerlessness I felt at having a tyrant for a president, and it caused me to go into a physical fight-or-flight response while listening to and seemingly agreeing with Samantha's perspective.

Once I made the connection, I subtly inhaled for a count of four, then exhaled for a count of six. Inhaled for four, exhaled for seven. Inhaled for four, exhaled for eight. I felt my body begin to calm down. I noticed I could hear her words more clearly and that my stomach was starting to settle. I didn't comprehend anything she said while calming my nervous system, I simply nodded to let her know I was still engaged.

Dinner arrived and interrupted the conversation. Once our food was in front of us, we began talking about our beloved pets, leaving the topic of politics behind. I was grateful for the tools I'd learned over the years, tools that returned me to my body and allowed me to continue building a connection with someone who held values vastly different from my own.

The experience was profoundly eye-opening. If I could have a trauma response while simply listening to someone's vulnerable perspective, then the degree of societal disconnection we were experiencing at that time made sense. What if we were all just trying to allow ourselves to be seen and heard through vulnerable conversation, but it was those very vulnerable conversations that were causing triggers in the people we most wanted to know us?

It took everything in me not to go on the defensive or run away from Samantha. If I hadn't been trauma-informed, I might not have had the resolve to stay and continue to witness her vulnerability. If I'd gone on the defensive, her walls likely would have zipped right back up. Rather than continuing to be vulnerable, she'd have hardened against my attacks, making any potential connection impossible. Was this one of the deterrents that kept us from loving each other up close? From being vulnerable and allowing others to be vulnerable with us?

I unintentionally tested this theory a month later while staying at my mom and stepdad's house in Connecticut. It was no secret that Gary and I didn't agree on many things, but as long as we didn't talk about them, we got along great. On this particular evening, the kitchen grew quiet as I watched my boys rush downstairs to prop themselves up in front of the only TV available in the house after dinner. "More wine?" I heard Gary ask.

Gary, Mom, and I were sitting around the kitchen table and letting our dinner digest before cleaning up. Our conversation began relatively calmly. The next thing I knew, Gary and I were arguing heatedly over immigration.

"So you think we should just let anyone into our country, take all our jobs, use up all our funds?" Gary said.

"No, that's not what I'm saying. I'm saying that if I lived in a country that felt unsafe for me and my children, I'd sure as hell try to flee too," I countered. "And the fact that the very country they are running to is ripping their children away from them is unconscionable."

"What do you propose?" Gary challenged me.

"I'm not saying I have an answer. I'm saying that first we need to see them for the human beings they are and recognize that they're the same as us," I said in frustration.

"If they were the same, they'd see what they're doing is wrong and not try to force themselves into a country that isn't theirs," Gary huffed.

"But you aren't looking at *why* they're forcing themselves into a country that doesn't even want them. Could you fathom having to make a decision where you knew that a country that didn't want you was still the better option than the home you grew up in and was the only place you'd known?" I asked.

"So we have to make arrangements for everyone just because their country can't take care of them?" Gary said.

"That's not what—" I could hear my voice getting higher and louder before Gary cut me off.

"What about the kids in third-world countries? What about them? The ones that are starving?" Gary began to get emotional. "We can't save them all. It's all we can do to care for ourselves." His emotions spilled over in uncommon tears.

In a flash, all the anger I'd been holding deflated like a balloon. It wasn't that he couldn't see the humanity, it was just too hard to see all of it at once. To try to hold that much suffering was a heartbreak very few of us could bear. I was witnessing his breaking point. I was witnessing his capacity for care. We were arguing for the same thing.

"Oh my god," I said. "You get it. I didn't think you got it, but you do. It's all about love. You're holding your love for those children in third-world countries just the same as I'm holding that same love for the people crossing our borders. It's so hard. It's so hard to love so big." I cried my own big, fat, wine-induced tears. I still wanted him to see that the people at our borders deserved his love, too, but I got it.

It feels hopeless at times to see suffering yet feel powerless to do anything about it. Instead we derive our power from wherever we can get it. Sometimes it's in aligning ourselves with a power greater than ourselves, like a government that appears to be protecting its own citizens by cracking down at our borders.

I didn't agree with his perspective, but I connected with his feeling of powerlessness. We commiserated on the injustices in the world and grieved together for the suffering of others. In that moment, we let our disagreements dissolve and hugged deeply over the shared humanity we saw in each other.

Chapter Sixteen

It's impossible to walk through the world holding all the love for all of humanity all the time. It's too big. It's too heartbreaking. Instead we find a way to hold love for our community. Our people. Our family. Our friends. The tricky thing is that sometimes what we think is love is actually control, and many of us grow up not knowing the difference.

When I embarked on MYOH in 2011, my intention was to share love with the people in my community. But I found the strangers I met and hugged that year easy to love because I didn't know most of them. I could hold a version of them in my mind that was flawless, kind, compassionate, and loving. A version that didn't include the hatred, jealousy, betrayal, and pain-inflicting judgment we all hold and express at times in our lives.

I could pretend that the grocery store clerk I hugged wasn't going home afterward to beat their child for making a mess. I could pretend that the mail person wasn't waiting for a break to call the other woman. I could pretend that all bullies had been reformed, and trauma didn't cause them to steal, rape, or murder. I could believe they were worthy of love because they hadn't inflicted pain on me. But did I also believe that about Simon, the man from my church who inappropriately propositioned me in the coffee shop?

The same held true for my cross-country trip. It was easy to love someone I was only spending a short, intentional time with, especially when that intention was to share hugs. But did I find it easy to love the less-than-sober man who crossed my personal boundaries at the park in Arizona?

In some ways, I did. It was easy to believe someone worthy of love when I could love them from a distance, one so vast I expected I'd never see them again. That distance gave me time to offer compassion and mercy for a life I wasn't privy to. I could imagine they'd come from broken homes or abusive relationships. I could imagine they'd been caught in circumstances that left them fighting for survival and perpetuating the cycle.

What a privilege it was to be able to excuse someone's behavior from a distance in order to maintain my belief that everyone was worthy of love. Though I didn't know it yet, I needed to have that privilege. It was the only way I could believe that I, too, might be worthy of love.

Knowing that mid- to late-October could pose weather-related risks in the northern states, I decided to drive due south from Washington through Idaho, then across the southern portion of Wyoming to get to Colorado. I'd done my due diligence and knew that after a certain time of year, snow tires or chains would be required for travel, so I prepared a route that would avoid the need for them. I naively believed I'd avoided any dangerous delays once I crossed the border from Idaho into Wyoming.

I was traveling along Interstate 80 when I looked to the south and noticed dark storm clouds in the distance. I took a deep breath and caught the whiff of impending snow. The winds and my anxiety were beginning to pick up. I didn't have time to pull over and check the weather for fear that even the slightest delay would cause me to get caught in the storm.

It was then that I passed a sign that read, "In extreme weather and high winds, I-80 will be closed to all traffic." Was I headed for extreme weather and high winds? If I kept traveling I-80, would I encounter a closure and be stuck in an area where I knew no one and had no idea where to go? I needed options. Immediately.

I risked picking up my phone while driving and punched in Chris's number. "Pick up, pick up, pick up," I willed him to receive my plea telepathically.

"Hi. You've reached Chris's phone . . ." it said.

Shit. Maybe if he saw me call again he'd realize I desperately needed to talk to him. I hit redial, then the speaker button, so I could put my phone back down and keep both hands on the wheel. I needed to maintain control of Sally because the winds continued to increase.

Pleeeeeeeaseee pick up, I telepathically pleaded again. I feared that in the time it took to reach him, I'd pass an exit that could lead me down a safer road.

"Hi . . ." Chris's recording mocked me again. I forcefully disconnected the call.

Okay, he had to have seen that I called twice. He could be in a meeting, and I should give him a minute to call back. He will call back, I soothed myself.

One minute crawled by in a silence interrupted only by the howls of another gust of wind. Despite the chill in the air, my pits were sweating. Once more, I hit redial. *This has to get his attention. Calling three times in a row is an automatic signal that it's an emergency, right? I'd never interrupt his work day in such an annoyingly insistent way unless it was an emergency. He has to know that, right?*

The phone rang once, twice, and on the third time I knew. *Oh my god. He's not going to answer. What do I do?* I panicked.

In my state of emergency, I completely forgot this was one of the heated arguments we had often; my inability to reach him by phone when I needed him the most. I think it was because something inside me knew anger wasn't going to help in this moment, soothing would.

I willed myself to relax. *Maybe his phone is on silent because he's in a meeting. He'll see that I called three times and call me as soon as he sees it. I feel bad because he'll probably be in a panic, knowing I've got some emergency.*

I needed to think. I needed to figure out what to do next. My sister! She lived in Florida, but she could still access the weather in Wyoming and Colorado, where I was headed. She could find more information for me. The clouds menacingly drew closer. Aware of the risk I took every time I held my phone to call, I grabbed my phone once again and punched in Kim's number.

Ring. Ring. "Oh god. *Please* pick up!" I begged her. Ring. "Hi, you've reached Kim . . . "

I kept the phone up to my ear, praying she'd somehow still be able to pick up even though I'd already gone to voicemail. There was a whooshing in my ears blocking out most of her message.

"Have a super sparkly day," I heard the message end. Shit.

I dropped the phone, forgetting to press end. "What the fuck am I supposed to do?" I wondered aloud. In an intense moment of focus, I had the clarity to call Drew, the friend in Colorado I'd be staying with in two days. I picked the phone up from the passenger seat where I'd dropped it and finally ended the call to Kim. I called Drew next, along with a quick pleading thought for her to pick up. Ring.

"Hello?" a voice answered.

"Oh, my gosh. Hi. Is this Drew? It's Melinda," I said, my shoulders dropping in relief.

"Hi, Melinda! We're so excited to see you," she said.

"Yeah, me too. But I was wondering if you could do me a favor?" I asked. "I'm in Wyoming on I-80, and it looks like there's a storm coming in. Would you be able to look up where it's coming from or if I-80 is closed at all? I don't want to risk stopping to pull over because it looks like the storm is coming in fast, and I don't even know if I'd be able to connect to the internet."

"Oh gosh, Melinda, I'd love to help you, but I don't have access to the internet right now. I'll tell you, though, those storms get pretty nasty. They close down the highways because the trucks overturn with those high winds."

My hope sank like a pit into the depths of my stomach. I wanted to throw up. "Oh man. Okay."

"You know, if I were you, I'd probably find a place to pull over and stay the night, try again tomorrow," Drew said.

"Yeah, okay, I hear you. It's probably a good idea. Thank you," I said and hung up. I knew I had to stay safe, but staying the night in a hotel meant that I'd have to cancel my other host in Colorado for that evening because I couldn't push back everyone for the rest of the trip. I still had half the trip in front of me.

Before I could make a decision, the phone rang. *I knew Chris would call*, I thought. The name on my screen was Kim. Disappointment mixed with renewed hope and anticipation.

"Hey, what's up?" Kim asked from over a thousand miles away.

I started to cry, feeling comforted by the familiarity of her voice. "Kim, I don't know what to do," I said. "Can you please check the weather in Colorado and Wyoming and see if there are any road closures on I-80?"

"Why? What's going on?" she asked.

I filled her in through my tears on the conditions that were visible around me. "I'm also really scared and fucking pissed at Chris for not picking up."

"I can't really do anything about Chris, but let me see what I can find out about the weather," Kim said. "It looks like there's a road closure on I-80, but I can't really tell where it begins. It also looks like there's an exit coming up that will bring you south to another road in Colorado that'll get you where you need to go."

"Great!" I said, ready to change direction. "Please stay on the phone with me." I turned right off I-80 and stared directly into the storm. "I don't know, Kim. It looks like I'm headed for the storm going this way."

"Hm, let me see." Kim spent the next five minutes trying to help me understand where the storm was. "According to the weather report I'm looking at, the storm should be east of you."

"But Kim, I'm staring directly at it," I said, neither of us registering the fact that the direction I was headed in was east. My nerves were on edge. It took a few minutes before I realized it was the Nudge sending out a warning. I needed to pull over and figure out the safest plan of action.

After parking the car along the side of the road, I said, "I think I really need to take Drew's advice, turn around, and spend the night at the hotel I passed just off the exit." As soon as I made that decision, my heart rate finally slowed down—confirmation of what the Nudge thought was best.

"Yeah, that's probably a good idea. Please let me know when you get there," my overprotective older sister said.

"I will. I love you. Thank you." I hung up, and with no cars coming in either direction, I made an easy U-turn and headed back the way I'd come as snowflakes began softly falling on my windshield.

Unable to call the hotel and reserve a room because I didn't know its name, I prayed that rooms would still be available by the time I got there. I didn't know how busy they'd get during a storm. I pulled up to the front door, ran in, and confirmed they still had rooms, taking note of the Mexican restaurant located just off the lobby. At least dinner would be taken care of. I returned to my car and moved it to the closest parking spot next to the front door.

As soon as I opened my door, it was ripped out of my hands by the wind. I stepped out, and my hair whipped around me, stinging my eyes. With effort, I closed the door and clumsily walked toward the back to get my luggage. The snow was still only falling lightly. It was the wind that was so brutal.

I walked as quickly as I could to the front door of the hotel without losing my balance or having one of my bags ripped out of my hands. I could only imagine the state my hair must've been in when I entered the building, but I didn't have any free hands to tame it, so my wild hair and I just kept plodding forward.

My phone rang just as I was approaching the counter. I thought it might be Drew wondering what decision I'd made, or Kim wondering if I'd made it to the hotel. Then it hit me like a ton of bricks. It was Chris—over an hour too late.

Fuming, I realized that even if I weren't carrying all my bags and had easy access to my phone, I still wouldn't pick up. I ignored his call, put my bags down by the front desk, and checked in, receiving a key for a room on the second floor. The lobby had floor to ceiling windows framing a darkening gray sky, but I was safe. "Let the storm roll in," I thought.

I walked toward the elevators while practicing breathing techniques so I'd have a clearer mind to talk to Chris. I just wasn't ready yet. In my room, I left everything packed, sat down on the floor, and began making calls. My first was to cancel with my host for that evening, Dave. Next, I called Kim to let her know I'd secured a room at the hotel so she wouldn't worry. Then I called Drew to let her know I was still on schedule to see her, but that I had taken her advice and decided to stay in Wyoming. Finally, it was time to listen to the message Chris had left.

"Hey. I'm sorry I missed your call. Call me back when you get a chance," the recording said.

I'm sorry I missed your call? Not, "Holy shit! I saw you called three times! I hope you're okay! I'm really worried, please call me as soon as you get this"? What the fuck? Was I a business partner or his wife?

All I could think was that if this were him away on a trip, I'd be freaking out. I wouldn't let my phone out of my sight. Didn't he realize his wife was by herself on a long cross-country trek where anything could happen? For all he knew, I could've been in an accident, and all he could say was "sorry I missed your call?" So much for calming down.

"Hey! What's going on?" Chris asked as soon as he answered the phone. "I saw you called."

"Yeah. Three times," I said, acid dripping off my tongue.

"I'm sorry, I didn't have my phone with me and I'd been in a meeting," he explained.

"You didn't have your phone with you?" I goaded him. "Your wife is clear across the country on her own, and you didn't have your phone with you?" My tone was as icy as the ground outside my window.

Chris remained silent.

"I needed you. I was scared and I needed you," I said.

"Well, what happened?" he asked, his own disdain barely hidden.

"Kim helped me, so I guess it doesn't really matter," I said through clenched teeth. If I didn't maintain that anger, I'd completely lose myself to heartbreak. While this particular situation was new, the argument wasn't.

We launched back into our well-rehearsed accusations of me being mad at him for not being accessible and him telling me it was out of his control. He argued that he couldn't know I was calling if his phone wasn't on him. I heard him say for the millionth time that he didn't know why, even when it was, it sometimes didn't ring. He'd tried. He'd really tried, he pleaded.

The argument escalated as I expressed my fears over not being able to rely on him for future trips. His answer to that was: "I'm not sure I want a wife who travels so much." His words smacked me in the face.

"What?" I asked.

"I just don't know if I want a wife who isn't around."

"But you know I love to travel," I said softly. "I've talk-ed about wanting to travel for speaking gigs, it's a dream of mine." I'd brought up the topic in conversation over the years ever since I'd declined blogging about travel days before starting MYOH because of my fears of what it would do to our marriage. When he didn't reject the idea, I kept dreaming about the day I'd make it a reality.

"Well, I just don't know if that's okay with me." He met my softness with his own.

I didn't understand why this was the first time I was hearing this. I'd thought he understood this was my dream. Why hadn't he expressed his feelings about it be-fore now?

"Then I guess we have a lot to talk about when I get home," I said, eager for the conversation to be over. I wasn't yet ready to face the reality that travel might real-ly be the catalyst that ended our marriage.

"I guess so."

We ended our call with the obligatory *I love yous* be-cause we did still love each other, I hoped. I dropped my phone beside me on the floor, put my hands over my face, and sobbed.

Eventually I had to grab a tissue so I could clear my nose enough to breathe. It was just the momentum I needed to drag myself off the floor and clean myself up for dinner. I tucked away my conversation with Chris in a sealed corner of my brain. I still had two weeks left of my cross-country trip. I couldn't let our conversation derail me.

On my way down the spiral staircase in the middle of the hotel lobby, I made note of the gray storm outside, snow swirling about in patterns as erratic as my emotions. I decided to spend the evening drowning my sorrows in burritos and Mexican beer. The next morning I'd compose myself, find a way to fill myself with the love I was out here to share, and complete my journey.

The next night while I acquainted myself with Drew's cats, she excitedly shared an invitation she'd received to spend a year in Europe on an archaeological dig.

"Oh wow! You'll be gone a whole year? What does Fred think about that?" I asked.

She gave me a look like she couldn't understand why I'd ask that question. "Oh, he supports me in anything I do."

From the corner of the kitchen where I didn't know he'd been listening, he concurred. "Oh yeah, I couldn't ever imagine not supporting her in doing the things she loves. I'll miss her, but it's her dream."

Thankfully the previous night's argument was still safely contained in that sealed corner of my brain or else I might have completely lost it in that moment. Instead I smiled sweetly, relishing in the love being shared with me as an example of what could be.

Chapter Seventeen

Over the course of the cross-country trip, I witnessed so much care, love, and support in the relationships of the people I stayed with that I began to believe those things might be possible for me too.

In Cincinnati, after spending a dream-filled day at the zoo where Audrey, my host, worked, she took me out to dinner with her kids at their favorite Italian restaurant. The scent of garlic and herbs filled the air, making my hunger spike as we waited to be seated.

"What's your favorite meal here?" I asked Audrey's daughter, Mia, once we were seated. At fourteen years old, Mia had extensive knowledge about the animals in the zoo and had given me a unique personal tour.

"Fettuccine Alfredo. I get it every time," she answered. And although it'd been years since I'd allowed myself the decadence of such a creamy pasta dish, I found myself ordering the same.

Most of the conversation at the table centered around Mia and her teenage brother, Jackson, their full lives ahead of them and their dreams still vividly possible. We were in the midst of conversation when Mia blurted out, "Well, I came out as gay when I was eleven."

"How brave of you," I said. "Do you want to share more?"

"Yeah, well, my mom and friends were super supportive, so it didn't feel like it was all that big of a deal," she said between mouthfuls of pasta.

Her mom gave me a knowing smile. "Of course I would always accept her no matter what." Looking over at Mia, she added, "You're my daughter and I love you." Jackson simply continued to shovel food in his mouth like the conversation was as mundane as the weather.

I marveled at the acceptance and love at that table, acceptance and love in which I felt included despite being a relative stranger. In that moment I felt safe and free to be exactly who I was. I knew that the barriers I had in place to protect the vulnerable parts of me wouldn't allow that to happen, but it didn't matter. I couldn't unknow the feeling.

I slept deeply that night on a mattress that felt like a cloud in a home that was filled to the brim with the clutter of life. Sometimes the least put-together and organized homes were the ones that felt the most inviting.

On the next day's drive to Asheville, North Carolina, I wondered if I'd been witnessing reality on this trip or if everyone was just on their best behavior. I already knew that it was easy to love others from a distance, and in the same way, it was easy to assume the best when the interaction was brief and temporary. It was time once again to put love in action—up close.

My final stop before home was my former place of residence—Raleigh, North Carolina, where thousands of people had shown me just as many different expressions of love through MYOH. They showed me vulnerability, courage, acceptance, peace, and of course, the physical act of wrapping their arms around me.

I wouldn't be hugging strangers again, but I'd get to spend quality time with my best friends. These were friends who I still talked with weekly even after I'd moved to Atlanta, which felt supportive after all other friendships I'd had up until that point seemed to dissolve after I moved away.

Eleanor met me outside her house as soon as I arrived. Her hug was as big as her love, and we stayed in our embrace for the full twenty seconds it took to allow the beneficial oxytocin to flood our bodies. With our stress levels reduced and feel-good hormones flowing, we walked through her front door to greet her large goofball dogs.

"Were those balloons outside for me?" I asked Eleanor once we'd settled into the house.

"Of course!" she said.

I smiled at the perfection of a trip bookended with celebratory balloons by two hosts who didn't know each other at all.

Eleanor and I went to Regina's house late the following morning to honor my journey with ceremony. In no hurry, we meandered through the woods behind her neighborhood. The path we found was just wide enough to accommodate Regina's son, Nathan, in his stroller. We collected feathers, unusual stones, heart-shaped leaves, and acorns. We stopped to watch butterflies. We marveled at the overhanging rocks that surely housed fairies.

I felt the back pocket of my jeans to make sure the folded piece of paper with my ceremonial outline was still there. With impeccable timing, we arrived at a clearing by the river just as Nathan settled down to nap. "I'm going to place sticks in an open-ended circle for the ritual to close out my cross-country trip," I said, arranging the sticks as I'd been shown during the ceremony weekend in New York.

Next, I directed my friends to their places within the circle. "We can keep Nathan by the entrance so he's included. Then, once we're in the circle, I'll guide us through the rest of the ritual."

With intention, I slowly entered the circle. I didn't actually have a clue what I was doing, but it felt important. All around us, birds sweetly chirped, the river softly bubbled, and the breeze danced to a harmony only it could hear. We completed the ritual with our arms wide open to the sky, inviting in the blessings of nature.

Suddenly, we heard a loud, "Mom?" We looked over at Nathan, sitting up wide-eyed in his stroller, and burst out laughing. The spell of the sacred ceremony was broken. When I left Raleigh a week later, I felt closer than ever to these women with whom I'd formed a spiritual bond.

As I headed home, I pulled over near the Georgia state line to take my picture at the welcome sign, as I had with every state I'd traveled. The picture showed a woman who was proud of her accomplishment, grateful to be returning home, and nervous about what was to come.

It was a Wednesday when I arrived home. The kids had school and Chris had work, yet I was still disappointed by the lack of fanfare when I pulled up. I took a few selfies walking toward my front door to commemorate the moment for myself. It seemed that life had returned to normal, except I felt like I couldn't return to normal.

I'd changed in ways I wasn't able to articulate yet, but I wasn't sure I fit into my old life anymore.

* * *

Buoyed by the holidays approaching, I threw myself into the distraction of decorating and shopping. I spent weeks perfecting the gift I gave Chris every year: an entry in our personalized, leather-bound journal. While I thought about what to write, I reread the previous two years' entries. Then I found the next blank page and wrote at the top: *50 Reasons This Year Was Great*, followed by a list all the reasons we had to be grateful. I opened my calendar to remind me of the events we'd attended. I thought back on all my favorite memories. I reminisced about that year's accomplishments and filled the pages with all the love I had to give.

In those weeks leading up to Christmas, I forgot most of our troubles. I forgot how abandoned I felt in Wyoming. I forgot that he didn't want a wife who traveled. I forgot most of the unresolved arguments we'd had over seventeen years together.

On Christmas morning, Chris inspected all his gifts, looking for the journal so he could put it aside as the last gift to open like he always did. It was the one he knew would be his favorite. As he read that year's entry, tears sprang to his eyes, and I thought I saw him forget all our unresolved troubles too.

"Three months. That's how much time I'll give myself to try one last time to turn this marriage around," I told myself at the beginning of January when our struggles resurfaced. I knew at that point I couldn't change him to be more like I needed, nor should I try.

We had both become so bitter and resentful that our relationship had turned into what professional marriage therapists John and Julie Gottman called a marriage of contempt. We both felt "right" in our positions of conflict, and knew just what to say or do to hurt the other. Of course, in those moments, it didn't feel like contempt. It simply felt like I wasn't being seen or heard.

Over those next three months, I became more aware of my contempt and painfully swallowed my words to keep the peace. I thought if I were more loving toward him, it would soften the edges of our conflicts enough that he might join me in that kinder space. Not only did that not happen, but the words that I swallowed fueled a slow fire that burned pieces of me away until I feared I would become nothing but ash. No doctor would've confirmed it, but I knew I was dying. Still, I stuck it out for the full three months.

When I'd been diagnosed with multiple sclerosis at age twenty-four, Chris saved me. He told me he'd always take care of me. He did his best to maintain that savior role, while I unconsciously embodied the role of damsel in distress even after I healed. We tried everything we could, for seventeen long years, to make our savior/damsel in distress relationship work and keep our marriage intact. Instead we had become roommates who didn't even like each other very much.

I had no idea if there was someone out there who would support and love me the way Drew and Clarissa's husbands supported and loved them, or even how Lynn and Jenny supported and loved me at the retreat in New York. But now that I knew it was a possibility, I wouldn't settle for less.

At the end of March, when my self-imposed three months were up, Chris discovered he'd been potentially exposed to one of the first cases of Covid in our area. He was quarantined for two weeks while the world shut down and his birthday approached. He spent those long days in his office, a converted bedroom with a small half-bathroom. The kids and I left food for him outside the door and washed everything he touched as soon as he was done.

With no symptoms to speak of after almost a week of quarantine, I took my chances and entered his space. "Can we talk?" I asked.

"Yeah, sure," he said, sounding defeated.

I wondered if perhaps he sensed what was coming. I sighed and said, "This isn't working. Us. We aren't working." I couldn't believe I was doing this days before his birthday while he was isolated from his family and the rest of us were shut off from the world, but I couldn't stop myself.

"What are you saying?" he asked.

I knew he knew what I was saying, but perhaps he needed to hear it out loud. "I want a divorce," I said, the words slipping out of my mouth like sand through a sieve.

He dropped his head. I didn't know if he was crying. I kept my head held high and allowed the tears to flow freely down my face.

After an undetermined amount of time, he lifted his head and with dry eyes confirmed, "If you hadn't said it, I would've."

"We've tried for so long and so hard," I said. "Seventeen years is a long time to try to make something work.

We just need to accept that it's not and likely won't ever work."

He nodded in agreement, and we fell into an uncomfortable silence. I watched him stare blankly ahead and wondered what he was thinking. "I mean, it's not like I can go anywhere right now anyway, so until the lockdown is lifted, we'll have plenty of time to figure out our next steps," I said, trying to manage the discomfort.

With a silent chuckle, he agreed.

"I don't think we should tell the kids until one of us is leaving the house," I said, continuing my attempt to mitigate the moment. Years before, we'd spoken to a therapist about what to say to the kids if we ever got divorced, and this felt aligned with what she'd shared.

"Yeah, that's probably a good idea."

"These next few months are going to be tough," I admitted.

Another silent chuckle. "Yeah."

As I walked out of his makeshift living quarters, I knew this decision was the most loving thing I could do for both of us.

The next three months were actually relatively easy. Without the pressure of making our marriage work, Chris and I could support one another through the terrifying first months of Covid as friends. We got along better than ever, but inevitably action would be required for dissolving our marriage. I didn't know how we'd separate, but I never questioned that I'd be the one to go. I just needed to figure out how we'd make that work. Chris's pay was cut drastically during the pandemic, and I knew we couldn't afford rent in addition to the mortgage on the house I was leaving.

I turned to my family. "Kim? Do you think I could come stay with you for the summer?" I asked my big sister.

Kim agreed to let me stay with her in Tampa, about a seven-hour drive from Atlanta. Chris and I decided to share custody of the kids in two-week cycles. We told the kids and explained that we'd meet halfway, in Valdosta, every two weeks for the swap.

Over the next few weeks, I packed up my belongings and stored most of it in the waterproofed section of our basement while the kids finished out their virtual schooling at the dining room table. The only belongings I took with me were my computer, a few books, three or four outfits, and my personal hygiene bag.

The ride to Florida on the day I moved was blurry. I kept the radio off and drove in silence, except for the sound of my sobs. I was grateful we decided to have the kids stay with Chris those first two weeks because I was a mess.

I'd desperately wanted us to work, and while I believed it was possible for me to find a better match, someone who would support and love me the way I needed, I wasn't sure I believed that I would. *Why did I just throw away my family? Why couldn't I just stick it out? Why couldn't I make it work? What could I have done differently?* I chided myself over and over again.

I repeated to anyone who would listen, "It doesn't make sense. It just doesn't make sense. Chris and I are perfect for each other—on paper."

Brené Brown teaches that relationships thrive when vulnerability is present. I didn't have a lot of experience asking for what I needed—that was the ultimate act of vulnerability to me—but I knew I needed emotional support throughout my divorce.

Regina, Eleanor, and I continued to stay in touch through regular bimonthly phone calls. During one of those calls, I risked asking for help. "Hey, do you guys think you can check on me more often? I'm really struggling with my emotions and I'm falling into pits of despair. I need you guys most when I'm in the pit, but when I'm there, I don't have the bandwidth to remember to call you. Even if I did remember, I don't think I'd actually have the energy to make the effort."

I felt embarrassed. It was ridiculous that I needed that. I didn't want to put another responsibility on their overly full plates just because I was struggling. We were all struggling in our own ways. I wanted to take it back immediately.

But they agreed. "We can definitely do that for you," Eleanor said.

I cried tears of both shame and relief.

A week later, relocated to my temporary home in Florida, I hadn't heard from either of them. Nine days later, still nothing.

I texted them: "Hey Regina and Eleanor. I'm feeling hurt. I shared a need I had in my time of grief with the divorce, and neither of you have reached out since. I know things come up, but I just wanted you to know how I was feeling."

I had no idea what I was doing. I'd never expressed my feelings that vulnerably before. I didn't know if I was doing it right, but I wanted my relationships to reflect the ones I'd witnessed on my journey and the only way I knew how to do that was try something new.

My vulnerability felt like a rooted seedling ready to grow. The right conditions, and it would develop a necessary outer shell to protect it from the judgments of others. The wrong conditions, and it could wilt, afraid to ever be seen again.

Almost immediately, I received a voice message back from Regina. "What do you mean you're feeling hurt? How have I not been there for you? This week was crazy, and I'm completely overwhelmed. Nathan's still not sleeping and barely taking naps during the day, and Bella [her daughter] is lashing out at me all the time. I don't need this from you too."

My vulnerability wilted. I called her back, hoping to clear up any misunderstanding.

"Hey," she answered curtly with an edge to her voice.

"Hey! I wasn't accusing you of anything. I was just letting you and Eleanor know how I feel." I immediately blurted this out with exaggerated enthusiasm to diffuse her anger.

"Yeah, well, I can't help you with that," she said. "I'm so overwhelmed. I need you to understand that I'm not always going to do exactly what you ask."

"But that's not what I'm saying. I'm saying that it was scary to ask you to check in on me in the first place, and when you didn't, I felt vulnerable and unimportant," I tried explaining.

"Well, that sounds like something you need to work on," she said. "I've always been there for you, and it feels pretty shitty that you can't see that and understand where I'm coming from."

My eyes briefly squeezed shut as I tried to understand what was happening. "But I wasn't even saying it was all you. I said it to both you and Eleanor, and I didn't say I was mad, just that I was sad," I tried explaining again.

The rest of the conversation continued to loop, each of us trying to get the other to understand our point of view. Our voices rose in volume until I met her anger with my own.

Luckily, I hadn't made it far on the walk I was taking when I'd called, and the only living things around that could hear our screaming match were lizards taking cover under thick, prickly foliage and birds calling out to one another in warning. The call abruptly ended with words I no longer remember, but I knew our friendship had ended.

I sobbed as I ran back toward Kim's house. She was outside giving much-needed attention to her beloved but often neglected plants. As soon as she heard me she dropped everything and came running. She gathered me up in a secure, protective hug, unaware of what happened but innately knowing what I needed. She gripped me tight, and I knew she wouldn't let go until I was ready. My face was hot and wet with tears that then dripped off my face and onto her shirt.

After a few moments, my screaming sobs morphed into softer wails that seemed to last an eternity, but she never let go. When my exhaustion finally grew stronger than my grief and confusion, my wails turned into soft whimpers, and I lay my head on her shoulder.

Lacking the strength to lift my head, I attempted to speak with my jaw resting heavily on her bony shoulder. "I think Regina and I just broke up. I don't understand. Just when I need her the most, I lose her?" Tears were beginning to flow anew. Kim wordlessly acknowledged my pain with another squeeze. "I mean, I just lost my husband, now I've lost my best friend too?" I cried.

Kim relaxed her grip on me without letting go. She pushed me out in front of her firmly but gently, so she could look directly in my eyes. "Fuck her. If she can't be there for you right now, then you don't need her. Fuck her," she said, giving my vulnerability the validation I needed to strengthen again.

My eyes widened in surprise, and I felt the giggle bubble up from the same place my anger and grief had just been. Kim giggled along with me for a few seconds, which was all we had capacity for. "Seriously, Melinda. You don't need this right now. If she can't see that, then maybe she wasn't as good of a friend as you thought."

I dropped my head down and stared at the ground. "Yeah, maybe," I said not quite believing it, but not really sure what to believe in that moment.

"Seriously. I don't know what she said, but if whatever it was made you feel like *this*, then she doesn't sound like a very good friend."

It made perfect sense, and even though I didn't want it to be true, I knew she was right.

I didn't really know what it looked like for a friend to be supportive through the most difficult times in my life because I hadn't really had anyone show up for me that way. But if the hug journeys had taught me anything, it was that there really were people out there willing to go out of their way to make the people they loved feel heard, seen, and valued.

In my darkest hour, Regina offered me none of that. As much as I wanted to be able to say that she just wasn't a good friend and let her go, I couldn't help but wonder if I was the problem in the first place. Had I been a good friend to her through her moments of need? If I continued to have friendships that crashed and burned at the first sign of trouble, which is what seemed to always happen, then wasn't *I* the common denominator?

When I hadn't heard from Eleanor by the next day, I reached out to clear the air with her too. "Hey, I'm sorry if I offended you with my text," I said as soon as she answered the phone.

"Huh? What do you mean? You didn't offend me, I just felt guilty for not being there like you asked," she said.

"Well, I didn't mean for you to feel guilty," I said.

"I know. That's just my own stuff," she said.

I noticed we were still talking about her feelings. "Have you heard from Regina? We got into it pretty good yesterday."

She hadn't, so I gave her an abridged version that evoked only a few tears.

"Oh, Melinda, that sounds painful," she said. "I can see how that would make you feel hurt and angry. I'd feel that way too. I'm sorry we weren't there for you like you asked." She used the right words to validate my experience, but rather than feel comforted, I felt even more disconnected from her. It was like she was reading her response from a handbook on how to comfort a friend in distress. I thought I remembered her saying she'd talk to Regina, but I wasn't exactly surprised when I didn't hear back from either of them.

I was at a loss. Had I been wrong? Was I not meant for those loving, supportive relationships like I'd seen during my hug journey? I had suspected I was going to lose my relationship with Chris, but Regina and Eleanor? They were the most supportive relationships I'd had beside my sisters—or so I thought. Was I so easily expendable that asking for support made them no longer want to be friends with me? Would I ever find someone who accepted me for who I was? Would I ever find friendships that would continue to be there for me regardless of distance, differences of opinions, or when I made mistakes? I was terrified I was destined to spend a lifetime building relationships only to have them fall apart again and again. I didn't know how many more times I could endure that heartbreak.

I spent a long time mulling over the possibility of moving to Connecticut or Florida just to be near at least one of my sisters, who I knew would never abandon me.

Chapter Eighteen

It would take most of the next two years to process all I'd experienced during MYOH and the cross-country trip. I wanted to expand this new perspective into one that allowed me to create the future I'd always wanted. I thought I knew what that looked like, but life still had tricks up her sleeve.

After almost three months in Florida, I made plans to move back to Georgia for the start of the school year. Apartment hunting wasn't easy in the midst of the pandemic, but Chris let me stay with him until I found my own place. Every day when I drove out of the neighborhood, I'd lovingly gaze upon the triplex at the top of my street and wish one of those apartments would become available. If I stayed in the neighborhood, the kids could walk back and forth between our houses, and I'd remain in the place I'd grown to love.

We lived inside the perimeter of Interstate 285, which was technically inside city limits. From my house, I could hear traffic on the highway and the train that blared its horn day and night. There were tanker trucks that illegally drove down the road at the top of our street, adding to the noise that proved our proximity to Atlanta. Despite all that, it felt like the closest to country living we could have found in the city, with a local park and hiking trails that led down to the Chattahoochee River just steps from our door.

We chose that neighborhood because it felt safe. It allowed us to give the boys the freedom to walk alone to their friends' houses. I even encouraged them to explore the woods beyond the train tracks. Back there along the trails, I saw deer, raccoons, turtles, and so many other animals. I'd hoped the boys would find as much joy and wonder in coming across them as I did.

I couldn't imagine giving that up, but as far as I knew, the people living in the triplex had been there for ten years or more. I couldn't imagine they'd leave any time soon, so off I'd go on a hunt for whatever apartment was available in my price range—which weren't many, if I wanted to stay in the same school district.

After an exhaustive search, I settled for an apartment about ten minutes away. It was outside the kids' school district, and I wasn't looking forward to driving them to school every day once the pandemic was over and school was no longer virtual, but I'd find a way to make it work.

I added my signature to the bottom of a lengthy lease, rented a U-Haul, and prepared to move my few belongings the next weekend. Even though Chris planned on helping, I still hired a few men to help me move and reassemble two beds, two chairs, and a small table along with the boxes I'd stored in the waterproof basement.

On the day of the move, I noticed there was no lock on the sliding door to my second-floor porch, wires were exposed in the shared bathroom, and the light in that bathroom didn't work. I immediately emailed the leasing agent at my complex and requested these items be completed before my children moved in two weeks later. I hit send just as the movers knocked on my door.

Once the furniture was in and assembled, the men began bringing in my boxes, holding the bottoms very gingerly. I cocked my head in curiosity and gave one of the boxes a once-over. A water stain was etched into the bottom of the box, and just under the stain was a hint of green.

"Oh my god! Don't put that down. Let me see that box!" I yelled, startling the man holding it. I walked over, bent down, and scrutinized the water stain. As he continued to hold the box, I pulled open the cardboard flaps and stared down at my collection of shoes in horror. Fuzz covered everything. "Oh my god! This box got wet. It's completely moldy! My shoes are ruined!"

I looked around frantically. "Don't put any of the boxes down!" I continued yelling. I saw a box already placed in the middle of the living room. "Pick that back up. I don't want any of that mold getting into my new apartment!"

All the boxes were brought back outside for inspection. I knew I was being hysterical and probably overreacting, but I had a friend who got horribly sick because of mold. My health anxiety was on high alert. I opened each box one by one. Books, more shoes, clothes, artwork, picture frames, hair supplies, journals, mementos—all ruined.

We put all the boxes in Chris's car and drove them the short distance to the building's communal trash bin. By the time I got back to the apartment, the men I'd hired had left, and it was time to return the U-Haul. Chris and the boys followed me. After I put the keys in the drop box, I joined Chris at his car.

I asked him what happened. "I don't know," he said. "The basement flooded like it does maybe once or twice while you were gone, but I didn't think to check the waterproof area. That area's never gotten wet before."

"I know. I know. How do you think it even got wet in there?" I said. "Maybe there was a leak somewhere else? That was a good four inches of water judging by the water stains on my boxes."

"I don't know. I'll take a look when I get home," he said before asking if I wanted to join him and the boys for dinner.

"No, thank you. I think I just really need to be alone tonight." I was unwilling to think about what just happened, but knew I'd have to deal with it as soon as I got back. I ran around his car, opening the back doors to give my boys a hug and kiss goodbye. "I love you, buds. I'll see you later," I said, trying to keep my emotions from spilling out and causing them any extra worry.

Back at the apartment, I sat down on the carpet in the middle of my living room and cried. Nearly all my worldly possessions were gone, my husband was gone, my friends were gone. I felt gutted.

Over the next two weeks, I began working as a receptionist at The Village Vets and making the best of my apartment. I arranged my few pieces of furniture in the living room and added flowers to the table by the front door. I got excited about making new recipes again as I put away all my cookware. Finally I added a cozy chair to my porch overlooking the residents' dog park, eager to get to know my neighbors' pets.

I hadn't yet gotten a mattress, so even though my bed frame was up, I had to sleep on the floor. Early one morning, I woke to the sound of screaming. An all-out battle had broken out below me. I looked at my clock. It was 3:30 a.m.

The yelling was epic. I couldn't make out what was being said other than the occasional "fuck" or "fuck you," but the malice in their voices was clear. Unsure if I should call the police, I listened for the unmistakable sound of physical violence, which fortunately never came. I hoped it was just a one-time thing.

The kids wouldn't be sleeping on the floor of their room, but I wondered how much of these arguments they'd still hear. In that moment, I didn't know how I was going to make this place a home for us. Along with the loud neighbors, the sliding glass door still didn't have a lock and the bedroom light was still broken.

When I headed back to my old house to assess the damage caused by the flood and take pictures for the insurance claim, I noticed a homemade sign posted at the top of my road. It was like a beacon of hope right there on the corner. "For rent," it said, and it was directly in front of the triplex I'd always admired.

That can't be right, I thought. It took me less than a breath to realize I didn't care if it was for the triplex or not, it was in the neighborhood I wanted to be in. I immediately texted for information, forgetting that I was already locked into a year's lease somewhere else.

"Hi. My name is Melinda. I saw the For Rent sign at the top of Whittier Ave. Is that still available and how many bedrooms is it?" I texted the number on the sign. Before I'd even finished parking at my old house, I'd received a text back.

"Yes, it is. It's two bedrooms, one bath," the response said.

"Great, can I come take a look?" I responded, remembering by this point that I was committed to a lease elsewhere but not caring.

Later that afternoon, I walked up to the triplex, where I met the landlord to see the apartment. We walked past the lush landscape the previous tenant had cultivated with both native and non-native species. At its heart was a huge succulent—the largest aloe-like plant I'd ever seen. Everything was mostly green, but I knew that in the spring the beds would be awash with color. We stepped through an arbor holding a climbing rose bush at the front of the porch before arriving at a brick-red front door.

Louis, the landlord, opened the screen door and put the key into the lock upside down, explaining that it was one of the many quirks of the place. Inside, it smelled like fresh paint and rich history. This home, like most of the others in the neighborhood, had been built in 1896 and was now preserved as a historical site. I felt at home with the weathered wood floor, outdated and unique coal fireplace, and textured ceilings.

We walked through the living room into a kitchen that felt like it belonged in the sixties or seventies with its avocado green cabinets and laminate countertops. Next, we backtracked through the living room to the first bedroom. The waist-high wainscoting along the living room walls continued in that bedroom. I noticed another coal fireplace beside the door to the second bedroom on the opposite side of the room. Once we entered the second bedroom, I realized that the bathroom was only accessible from that room. At first, I was so enchanted by the whole place that I didn't even consider that anyone who visited, including my boys, would have to go through my bedroom to use the tiny bathroom.

The next week, I was woken up two more times by the epic fights of the neighbors, and my apartment still wasn't fixed. I'd made up my mind. "Louis? I'd like to rent that apartment," I texted, not really caring how I'd get out of the current lease but hoping it would all somehow work out.

The kids arrived to spend their only two weeks in the first apartment amidst my flurry of emails breaking my lease and explaining I wouldn't be paying any lease-break fee because without the repairs, the apartment wasn't safe enough for me and my children. And that was true. But it was also true that the place I'd wanted all along had just become available.

After I moved into the triplex, I sat on the long front porch journaling and staring out at the incredible garden. In that moment, I knew I'd made the right decision despite any hit my credit score might take for the lease-break fee the first apartment would never collect.

It took power and courage to make such a bold decision. I wasn't willing to settle for what was available. Instead I said yes to a more perfect environment for me and my boys. The strength and audacity it took to take such action led me to believe I could do that in other areas of my life. I began noticing where else I was settling. The most obvious was the pittance I'd agreed to receive from Chris in a preliminary and unofficial divorce agreement.

A strength was rising in me, bolstered by the experience of witnessing the type of loving, supportive relationships I wanted for myself while on the hug journeys. A strength that refused settling for anything. A strength that didn't hide behind a victim story to claim my worthiness but rose like the Phoenix, transformed by the ashes of lies I no longer allowed myself to believe.

Chris and I agreed to file for divorce pro se—meaning we weren't involving lawyers or mediators. We trusted each other and believed in the friendship and communication we'd developed over the seventeen years we were together. Knowing the financial strain this divorce would put on both of us, my initial suggestion was for Chris to give me a monthly stipend that would barely cover my rent.

I assumed it was my responsibility to find a job and cover the rest of my own financial needs. While this was true, I also still viewed our marital financial assets as his no matter how many times he'd tried telling me otherwise over the years. It just didn't feel true. It wasn't until my head cleared from the noise and confusion of our years together that I realized why the money never felt like mine.

Despite trying to stick to a budget, we'd often lived close to or beyond our means. We'd splurged on expensive cruises. We regularly went out to eat at nice restaurants. We eventually even purchased season tickets for the Buffalo Bills so we could guarantee the seats we wanted for the one game we went to each year. While we did try reselling the rest of the tickets, there was no guarantee.

Yet when I approached Chris about needing money for the coaching program I wanted to take as an investment in the business I wanted to build, I got backlash. "We don't have money for that. We barely have enough money to get by. Isn't there something you could do to earn the money for that course?" he said. His arguments felt valid, so I didn't question them.

Eventually, I got my way, but only after pleading and making my case in much the same way I'd needed to with my neurologist when I wanted to come off medication for the MS. It never occurred to me to question why I had to plead my case for my own autonomy.

Shortly before asking for a divorce and in the midst of another money argument, something shifted. I viewed these arguments from the new clarity that came from seeing how people in other relationships supported each other. That day, I asked for money for something, maybe an overnight trip with my friends or an upgrade to my phone—the what was irrelevant. The argument, however, was the same.

"We're still living paycheck to paycheck. We don't have money for that," Chris said.

"What do you mean?" I argued. "We could just eat in for the next week or two instead of going out to restaurants, and that should cover it."

"Why should I have to deny what brings me pleasure just so you can get this?" he countered. "If you hadn't gone on that cross-country trip or taken that coaching course, we might have the money."

In that moment, it was like the clouds in my head parted, the sun shone through the bullshit, and the angels burst forth in song. Through clenched teeth and with my eyes squinted in slits, I said, "The cross-country trip didn't cost you one extra cent. My overnights and dinners were paid for. I received donations that covered my gas, lunches, and snacks. If anything, I saved you money that month."

My voice dripped with disdain; I'd finally had enough. I continued, "Why does it always come down to this? Why is it always my fault we're living paycheck to paycheck? I never hear you say, 'Well if we hadn't gone on that cruise or if we didn't go out to eat multiple times each week, we might have the money.' It's always the things that I did, the books I'm buying, the courses I'm taking, the organic foods I'm choosing. That's fucked up. No wonder I've spent years thinking our money isn't mine. I don't think you actually believe it is."

I fumed and stormed out of the room, letting that be my final say for fear that if he retaliated, I'd be persuaded to believe that once again I was in the wrong.

Chapter Nineteen

It takes time—years, sometimes—to extract yourself from beliefs and habits impressed upon you since birth, especially when those beliefs and habits are attached to your own safety and basic core needs like money security.

My belief in myself was growing. Each declaration of a need I had and each boundary I set in place fanned the flames of the growing power inside me. It was a power I was afraid to embrace because the only one I'd ever known was *power over*. I was about to discover the greater strength of *power within*.

When Chris and I first talked about separating, I continued to treat the money as though it was his. After all, he was the one going to his job day after day to earn it. Through that lens, I thought about his needs before my own. I wanted to be sure he was taken care of first, and I'd find a way to survive off what was left. Not to mention the fact that I refused to be one of those wives who "took him for all he was worth."

It would still be another few years before I understood the controlling lies of the patriarchy.

Naively, I believed he was considering my needs the same way I was his. When he agreed to pay me an amount that would barely cover rent, I assumed it was because it truly was the most he was capable of giving me so that he could keep our house in order to maintain a stable foundation for the boys.

That all shifted the day he approached me and said, "Hey. I can't keep the house. I've worked the numbers, and we need to put it on the market. If I can get an apartment, then we can split the equity, and we both should be able to stay in the same school district."

At first, it seemed reasonable. It took a couple of days for me to realize that he hadn't also discussed increasing the amount of monthly support he'd give me as he decreased the amount of money he'd need for his expenses.

Sometimes the dawning is a slow burn that simmers uncomfortably in the body, drawing in fuel for the moment when the pressure has built enough to explode. After losing nearly all my possessions, I had nothing left to do but surrender to this slow burn rising from within.

That day, Chris timidly stepped into my small, cozy apartment. I'd asked to see him without the kids. I continued to breathe deeply, knowing I wanted this difficult conversation to come from a place of power and kindness.

The pressure inside was at a tipping point, and I knew if I didn't manage my nerves, fear would replace power, and I'd approach Chris from a place of victimhood—a place that sometimes got me what I needed but never felt empowered.

Chris gave me a quick compulsory hug, then leaned over to pet my chihuahua, Tater Tot, who'd technically been a family pet but had claimed me as his person. I invited Chris to sit on my small, peacock blue couch while I paced back and forth, preparing myself to release the pressure inside in small doses. What I was about to say wasn't his fault. It wasn't mine, either, but I sure as hell wanted someone to blame.

First, I had to make my request. "I want half. Half of everything. Half of your monthly take-home pay, half of the 401K, half of the equity in the home after the credit card debt is paid off, and half of the stock options in your company."

I watched rage flash across his face for a split second before he regained the cool composure he was determined to walk through life with. I didn't expect him to say anything, so I filled the space with the injustice I'd come to discover that had fueled the pressure inside.

"While I don't blame you for my decision to quit college, I did so because you promised to take care of me for life even amidst my diagnosis," I said. "We got married to declare our love for one another and solidify this promise. We promised to love one another till death do us part. I know we still love each other, but that love has morphed, and neither one of us has died.

"Here we stand, at the edge of the precipice of a new life we must create for ourselves, and while it sucks that your life must change, you don't have to worry about how you will make ends meet. You have a well-paying job as well as skills you've continued to hone for twenty years that set you up for success even if you lose your current job.

"My life is also changing, but I don't have a degree to use to seek out a job in my field. I don't have experience in the workforce that will enable me to get a job for much more than the going minimum wage in our area. My lawyer has informed me that in Georgia, alimony is typically awarded for about three to five years max.

"So what I'm ascertaining from that is that I'm expected to climb my way up some corporate ladder in record time with minimal experience in order to come close to half of the salary we built together so I can maintain the life I've grown accustomed to. Or I can go back to school, putting myself in debt for a degree I may not be able to complete by the time my alimony runs out for a base salary that might be a third of the lifestyle I'm used to—if I'm lucky.

"Or that I just have to let go of the lifestyle I'd built and grown with you and settle for the crumbs others are willing to throw at me." I felt the heat inside me growing, leaving visible redness along my face and neck. "This system does not set me up for success while it allows you to continue to grow what we've built together—without me."

Here, I paused for a breath, then continued. "I may not have always kept the home neat and orderly, but without me you couldn't have worked the massive amounts of hours you did to help be part of the company you have risen to the top of. We did this together. You may have gone to the job, but I maintained our family, our home— hell, our marriage.

"I'm not asking for more than you'll be receiving. I'm not even asking you to give me half of your salary. I'm asking for half of your monthly take-home. Once we're divorced, your life will be different, but you won't have the added stress of wondering what the rest of your future holds and how you will make ends meet, whereas I'll have to find a way to build a future that you had twenty years and a supportive partner to build in just three to five years on my own." I finished with tears of rage, injustice, and fear leaking down my face despite my attempts at curbing them.

"Okay. I have to think about all this," Chris said with the same calm, cool composure that had always kept me in the dark about what he was thinking.

I believed he loved me, and I believed he'd understood the injustice I was talking about and would want to fight for me just as much as I needed to fight for myself. When he walked out the door without a hug, I wrapped my own arms around myself, feeling proud of my courage. Proud of my willingness to stand up for what I needed, and proud of my ability to not place blame on him but showcase the injustice of the society we lived in. I didn't know what would happen next, but I knew I finally had my own damn back.

A few weeks after the world shut down amidst the pandemic, a friend of mine in Atlanta, Kelbi, gathered together eleven women via text who knew one another through a spiritual women's group. We called ourselves the Coven. Through our text thread, we clung to each other desperately in those first months as we all navigated the fears, confusion, and despair of living in unprecedented times.

In the past, most of my friendships left me with an emptiness I couldn't explain. Inevitably, they would fall apart, but that didn't stop me from trying again. I needed connection. I needed to feel a sense of belonging. *What's wrong with me?* I'd wonder after yet another friendship collapsed. I'd always assumed I was the problem.

Determined to build a strong foundation with this group of women, I offered up my time and services to them. I held grief circles over Zoom and ensured that no text went by without my acknowledgment of it. I offered up as much of myself as I could until there was nearly nothing left to give. The divorce wiped me. The attempt at rebuilding my life wiped me. These new friendships were wiping me. I was so depleted, the only thing I had left to give was the raw, gritty, messy me.

"Hey, if anyone's around, I really need a friend," I texted the group, my face streaked with tears.

Starr was the first to respond and suggested opening Zoom so everyone could join. As much as I needed the connection, it felt too vulnerable to be seen in the state I was in. I nervously asked if we could keep the videos off. As soon as she agreed, I felt my shoulders drop.

I sent the Zoom invite to the Coven text thread, inviting anyone who was around to join. It was the middle of a weekday. I didn't expect the women to be available; jobs still needed to be attended to even amidst the shutdown, but at least Starr would be there. While Zoom was connecting, I grabbed the box of tissues on my nightstand and placed them on the bed next to me. I took two tissues, wiped my face, and blew my nose, trying to compose myself.

Holding my phone in my left hand, I watched Starr join the call, followed by Kelbi. I was still on mute and took a deep breath before announcing myself. "Hey," I said, masking my depressed state to the best of my ability.

"What's going on?" I heard Sydney say before noticing she'd joined the call too.

Unable to pretend to be anything other than what I was in that moment, I surrendered to my vulnerability praying it would be safely held by these women I was still getting to know. "I just can't anymore," I said, beginning to sob again and blocking up the nose I'd just cleared.

"Can't what?" a familiar voice I couldn't place asked.

"I don't know. Life? It's just too much. I don't want to be here anymore," I said, quickly following up with, "It's not that I want to kill myself—I don't think I'm suicidal, but I don't want to live. I don't want to human anymore. It's just too hard." I heard a collective, tense sigh of understanding, which made me cry even harder.

"It *is* hard, Melinda," Kelbi said after my sobs finally slowed down and my breath began returning to a somewhat steady rhythm.

"This sucks, Melinda," Starr said. "Everything has changed. You've lost your marriage, your home, everything you knew, all in the middle of a pandemic. It'd be a lot for anyone. It's a lot for everyone right now."

My heart lightened a bit.

"Fuck this world," Sydney added with her own flair. "It sucks to be human."

We all sat with the weight of these truths, not knowing yet that this moment was a preview of what was to come for two out of the three women on the call.

"It really does suck right now, but you're strong and you'll survive this. Not only will you survive, but you'll finally realize what a badass you've been all along," Starr said.

I chuckled. "I sure don't feel like a badass."

"No, I'm sure you don't, but you aren't giving up. And you were willing to reach out to us for support. That says a lot about your willingness to keep growing," Starr continued.

I took a moment and allowed myself to receive the love and support these women were offering me while we sat there in comfortable silence.

I don't know if it was my deep need to believe that people would be willing to show up for me or the fact that I had nothing left to lose, but I followed the silence up with a request. "Hey, do you think you guys could do me a favor?" I asked.

Even before they knew the request, I got murmurs of agreement.

"When I'm deep in pain, I don't have the energy or sometimes even the ability to remember to reach out to someone for help. I'm in deep pain often these days. Would y'all please check in on me every once in a while?" I vulnerably asked for what I hadn't received in the past, terrified of being let down again. I wasn't sure if I could survive this rejection again, but I knew with absolute certainty I wouldn't survive without at least trying. I felt buoyed when, over the next week, I heard from all three.

Maybe I needed to lose everything I had to build it all anew. Or maybe I'd simply held on to too many things I'd outgrown for too long, and my new life demanded a release of everything that kept me questioning my worthiness.

Chapter Twenty

I thought losing my husband, all my possessions, and my friends was the epitome of starting over, that it was my rock bottom. But something deep within me knew better. It knew I had to dig below that rock bottom to release the pressure from the countless lies I'd believed about myself. I cried hard and often in those years following my divorce.

On one particular morning, I started crying before the sun rose above the trees. I dragged myself out of bed, resigned to the fact I wasn't going to get any more sleep. I went for a walk in the neighborhood, and despite the early morning hour, the humidity was already stifling. I didn't bother wiping my tears, knowing no one was awake to see me. Not that I'd care. The pain in my heart threatened to overcome me; my tears were the only release valve I knew.

I threw my hands in the air, shouting out loud, "Why, God? Why am I here? I don't understand. Do you even know I'm here? I feel like you made a mistake with me. Everything about me is wrong. I can't find happiness, even when everything seems to be going my way.

There has to be something wrong with me. You must have made a mistake. I just don't understand. I don't want to be here anymore. Please just release me from this Earth. I have nothing to give, no one understands me, I am just too different. I'm certain you made a mistake when you made me."

My tears soaked my face and shirt, and I had to let muscle memory guide me in the direction I'd been taking twice a day for years. I didn't know what I wanted out of the walk. I didn't know what I expected to get out of sharing this pain with God and the trees around me. I just knew I couldn't hold it in any longer.

I climbed back into bed when I got home, preferring the escape of sleep over the soul-crushing experience my life had become. I slept on and off for the rest of the day, rising only to do the bare minimum necessary to keep myself and my pets alive.

At 3 a.m., I woke in another fit of angst. I tried to walk off the energy once again rising in me by taking my well-worn path around the neighborhood under the cover of darkness. Rather than releasing the energy, it magnified it. The judgments and beliefs of the previous morning increased in scope and intensity.

When I got back home, I collapsed on my bed and threw a tantrum bigger than that of any toddler. I had age, experience, and strength on my side, after all. Lying askew with my head toward the wall and my feet closer to the edge of the bed, I pounded my fists and kicked the mattress as hard as I could in that early morning hour, not even caring that I might wake my neighbor.

Raw, guttural screams emerged from my throat. I heard myself saying, just as I had at twenty-six when multiple sclerosis ravaged my body, "This is not my life. This can't be my life."

In that moment, I thought the amount of energy coursing through my body was going to kill me, but I knew I couldn't stifle it any longer. I let the rage, shame, and power surge up and express itself in this adult-size tantrum. If it killed me, so be it.

An undetermined amount of time later, the energy began to dissipate. The kicks and punches subsided. The tears dried up. I felt hollow—lifeless but not dead. I let my eyes close and drifted off into a restless slumber. When I woke, I still felt like an empty shell of myself. I just didn't care anymore. About anything. I walked the same route I'd walked in the early morning hours, shuffling my feet along listlessly.

I knew I didn't have anything pressing for the rest of that day except for a virtual healing session on Zoom with my energy practitioner, Nadia, who I'd met at church when I lived in Raleigh. I sat on the small couch in front of my TV and stared numbly at whatever mindless show I could find until it was time for our session.

Guided by love, Nadia often validated my pain, held space for it, and energetically helped lift that which no longer served me. This day was different. She was still guided by love, but it was tough love. "You need to stop, Melinda. You *have* to stop listening to the voice in your head. It's only delivering you lies and pain," she said forcefully. "I will not have you continue down this path. I know where it leads, and you are too important for that."

With a blank stare, I said, "Okay," not really believing that those voices I heard inside were lies. I didn't remember that just a few years before, I'd discovered that those voices were mean and bullying. They were voices that indicated a hatred for myself.

"You are not a mistake. You were divinely made and with a strong purpose. You've been a great blessing in my own life," she said.

"Okay," I said again, numb to her words of encouragement.

"Listen to me," she insisted. "You must listen to someone else's thoughts, anyone other than yourself for the next week. I'm not kidding. I want you to listen to Abraham-Hicks, Mooji, Joe Dispenza, Byron Katie, anyone but yourself. Find who you resonate with and only listen to them."

I was familiar with some of those names. I didn't bother writing them down.

"I'm serious. That's all I want you listening to 24/7. Put earbuds in while you sleep and continue listening even through the night. I don't want your own voice breaking through at all."

At this, a little life returned to my body. It felt relief at the thought of not having to listen to the terrible things I had to say about myself. I stared straight ahead at the unused computer monitor in front of me and realized I was sitting at a desk in my boys' room.

"Okay," I said, this time with a hint of conviction and hopefulness.

For the next three days, I did just that. I found Abraham-Hicks to be my preferred choice. When I needed to get things done around the house, I put my earbuds in, tucked my phone in my pocket, and kept listening. And, as suggested, I kept them in when I went to bed, willing to suffer through the discomfort of keeping them in overnight for the sake of listening to someone else's thoughts.

Hope reminded me of the curiosity I felt after the cross-country trip was over—a curiosity about what was possible. Curiosity fueled more hope. I had no idea what lay ahead for me, but through the words of Abraham-Hicks, I risked believing it could be something greater than I'd known before.

After three days, I felt strong enough to sleep without distraction, although I continued to listen to Abraham-Hicks throughout the day. After a week, my thoughts increased in positivity and possibility. I decreased the amount of time I listened to Abraham until I was only listening in the morning and any time the dark thoughts returned.

Abraham-Hicks's messages resonated so profoundly because they reminded me of who I was when I was younger. When I was a little girl, I knew the world was magical. I knew I was magical. I was different, and that's what made me special. I talked to animals. I communed with the trees. I found treasures along the river's edge. I felt big love for myself and everything in the world. I even manifested everything my little heart desired because I didn't know I couldn't.

When I was five, we attended mass at Sacred Heart Catholic church. During one of their fundraisers, they had a silent auction. My parents bought tickets, handed me five, then guided me to place them in the boxes next to the prizes I wanted to win. I placed all five in a box next to a small gold purse that was about the size of a deck of oracle cards. It had a gold chain and a gold kiss clasp. The inside was lined with gold satin. It was the most exquisite thing I'd ever laid my eyes on.

"Honey, you should have spread your tickets out so you had a chance of winning other prizes," I heard my mom say.

"Oh no. I didn't need to. I'm winning the gold purse," I confidently claimed. In my mind, the purse was already mine. Both of my parents chuckled at my innocent naivety and walked away to mingle with other parishioners. I stood by my purse for the rest of the fair. I didn't think about where I'd wear it. I didn't think about why I might need it. I simply coveted it for the sake of its shiny beauty.

When the time came for the winners to be announced, I reluctantly left the table to join my parents in the large crowd gathering in front of the tables. I only heard my name after I reached the table to take what was rightfully mine. When I looked back at my parents, I wondered why they looked so surprised. I'd already told them I'd win it. In those days, it was just as simple as that.

Abraham-Hicks's messages confirmed this ease I'd felt as a child. They confirmed the magic I'd felt all around me. They put into words the conditions of a universe that was guided by love and attraction—conditions I'd innately known as a young child but that had caused me to be perceived as an awkward outcast when I'd lived my life as though those conditions were true.

It didn't take long for me to learn that in order to fit in, I needed to change and not stand out. I learned that I needed to be more like everyone else. This is when I began telling myself stories about how wrong I was. About how broken I was. About how different I was than anyone else I knew, and how that difference kept me from fitting in with the human race.

But I was determined and excellent at observation. So when the girls in my middle school started rolling their jeans as part of the new fashion, I discreetly watched how they did it so I could do it too. When I noticed the smooth, hairless skin on their legs, I grabbed my dad's razor as soon as I got home and taught myself how to use it. When a popular girl in my science class turned around to declare her love for a boy in that same class, I determined that the right thing to do was make your intentions with the opposite sex known. I sent a flower-gram to a boy in my grade asking him to the next dance. I was elated when he said yes, but humiliated when he never showed.

Despite making tons of mistakes, my determination to get it right and behave like everyone else was strong. The only thing was, the more I behaved like everyone else, the farther I got from the truth I knew as a child. I stopped relying on the universe and my intuition and started putting my faith in others. I believed they knew better than me.

I couldn't have known at that young age that relying on others to show me how life was supposed to be lived would create an endless, exhausting pursuit of perfection. I couldn't have known I'd have to devote all my energy to honing my observational skills and making others' lives my own. I couldn't have known that once I perfected an acceptable image, I'd never be able to let the mask slip, and it would become my new identity.

When I discovered through trial and error that I was meant to be seen as a beautiful woman and nothing else, I was determined to be the most beautiful woman I could be. I wore the latest fashion that my budget could afford and faked it when I couldn't. I played up my most prominent feature, my hair, so that even if I didn't have the most up-to-date clothes, I could distract those around me with my full mane of red hair.

When I discovered that my body captured the attention of boys around me, I wore the skimpiest tops and tightest skirts. When I discovered that my opinions would be judged, criticized, and unwelcome, I became an observer. When I discovered that I wouldn't be taken seriously as a woman for my beliefs, dreams, and ambitions in life, I succumbed to being a supporting character.

This way of being was so fragile, all it took was one new judgment, one new invalidation, one new shameful comment to tear me down. These comments taunted me.

"Why do you wear that? You look like a slut."

"Eww, that Benetton shirt is so last season."

"Why did you cut your hair? It looked so much better the other way."

"How could you think that? Don't you know anything about the way the world works?"

"Come on. Very few people can make a living that way. What makes you think you can?"

Each cutting remark became another brick I added to the defensive wall growing around my heart. Behind it, I stored pent-up anger and rage at living a life others mapped out for me.

People accepted me when I played nice. When I did what they expected. When I played by their rules. When I ignored all my own needs for the sake of theirs. After living nearly forty years for other people's acceptance, something had to give. On the night of my tantrum, it did.

Within that first year after discovering Abra-ham-Hicks, it was enough just to listen to their wisdom and remember things long forgotten. Meanwhile, I welcomed the retreat from humanity during the height of the global pandemic. Sheltering in place, I sought refuge in nature.

I spent hours in the woods of Whittier Mill Park, renewing my relationship with the wilderness. I followed the trails to the brisk-moving Chattahoochee River and released everything that wasn't the authentic me to the wind. I leaned against the supportive, rough trunks of oak trees, soaking up their wisdom and care. I giggled each time an animal crossed my path. I remembered how much joy I got from giggling.

During that time, I rediscovered the clear language of nature. The birds sang to me. The raccoons invited me to play. The deer walked up to me with curiosity. That was where I'd always belonged. I didn't want to leave. The only humans I spoke to during that time were my Coven friends, my immediate family, and my boys. At a time when others floundered under the weight of an unsure future, I found peace and comfort in the opportunity to remember who I'd been as a child. The authentic me.

When the world finally felt safe enough for people to begin moving among themselves again, I was afraid. I wanted to remain in my little cocoon, in the safety of nature, where I knew who I was and how to be in the world.

I was terrified that by rejoining the world, I'd revert to habits that forced me to conform to a society that wasn't built for someone like me. Someone who relied on her instincts over knowledge. Someone who followed the Nudge in her gut even when it didn't make sense to anyone else. Someone who wanted to finally just be her weird, awkward self. Someone who was too tired of trying to be anything else.

I knew I was wired for human belonging and that I'd need to venture back out in the world eventually. But I was afraid that my need to belong would cause me to override my need to be authentic. I was afraid I'd find myself among people who wouldn't accept my wild, weird self and I'd once again conform to fit in. Fitting in led me to hit rock bottom, and it nearly killed me. I wasn't sure I'd survive that again.

Slowly, and with the encouragement of the friends I'd made through the Coven—friends who had yet to abandon me in my times of need or even my times of weirdness—I reentered the world. As Anaïs Nin said, "The day came when the risk to remain tight in a bud was more painful than the risk it took to blossom." I knew it was time to blossom.

Chapter Twenty One

When I embarked on MYOH, I was searching for my purpose in life. I was seeking to add value to the world, to add value to my family. The greatest value I had to give was my ability to love. I chose to share that love with hugs.

A hug can say a thousand different things with no words. I love you. I'm sorry. I'm so proud of you. I want to comfort you. I miss you. I need comfort. You make me happy. We belong together. I know you. I appreciate you. Hi. I'm relieved. I'm here for you. Congratulations. And so much more.

It's a language understood by everyone, whether they're a hugger or not. I intended for my hugs that year to say, "I see you. I appreciate you. You matter to me."

What I didn't know was that they were also saying, "Please see me. Appreciate me. Tell me I matter." I did receive immediate validation for the good work I was doing, but it was fleeting—love exchanged between two strangers who would never see one another again.

I loved so many people that year, but I didn't understand why at the end of it all I felt so empty, so alone. I didn't see that loving people from a distance without ever really knowing them was beautiful but hollow, just like Rebecca the Born-Again Christian Woman said in that email after MYOH was over. I needed to learn how to love people up close, but before I could do that, I needed to learn how to love myself up close.

After the extreme tantrum on my bed that fateful morning, I spent the rest of the pandemic learning how to choose a better life. Learning how to look in the direction of joy rather than pain and trauma. Learning how to accept and appreciate myself. In the comfort and safety of my home, I got pretty damn good at it. I didn't know if I'd be able to continue showing up that way out in the world, in the face of others' judgments.

In the summer of 2021, I drove down with the boys to visit my dad in Florida. I gripped the steering wheel tightly, a headache beginning to form from the way I clenched my jaw. I glanced over at my boys, but they were too busy watching YouTube to notice my tension. I was worried I'd fall back into old patterns, the ones that left me feeling powerless and like a little kid looking for Dad's approval. I didn't always agree with his opinions, but I was afraid to speak up. I didn't want him to think less of me for my opposing views. But the less I spoke up, the more distant we became.

When I discovered that he'd voted for Trump shortly after the 2016 election, I was dumbfounded. I didn't understand how the man who'd taught me to treat everyone with kindness and respect could vote for a bully to run our country. I didn't understand how the man who compassionately drove me to the doctor's office for my abortion had voted for a man who wanted to take that right away. I didn't understand how the man who befriended a young disabled boy that screamed with glee every time my dad came around could vote for someone who openly mocked the same kind of person.

Up until that point, I'd ignored my confusion and continued to love him to the best of my ability, but it was becoming increasingly difficult. It wasn't that I couldn't love him despite his having a different opinion than me. It was that I couldn't continue loving myself without having the strength to stand in my own opinion.

By 2021, Joe Biden had replaced Trump in office, but the damage had been done. Sitting at a picnic table in front of the RV where my dad and bonus mom, Nancy, were temporarily living, I listened uncomfortably as he made an off-putting joke reminiscent of ones made by Trump himself over the years. It was time to stand in my own truth. When Dad looked over at me, I stared back stone-faced, my discomfort revealed only in the unnoticeable shake of my knees.

"It's not okay, Dad," I said. "I've asked you not to make jokes like that in front of me. I'd rather you not make them at all. They aren't funny and they're offensive."

"Offensive to who? There's no one around here who'd be hurt by that joke," he chuckled , looking around like he was searching for someone who might be offended. His smile was meant to be disarming.

"Me. I'm offended by that joke," I said. "Every time you make a joke like that, you dehumanize someone, and that's hurtful." The nerves in my stomach were fluttering wildly. I'd never made such a bold statement to him before. Would I be strong enough to keep this from turning into a screaming match or worse, backing down from what I believed?

Dad raised his hands in surrender and turned back to the house project he was working on. There was no backlash. He didn't try to defend his stance. That was new. I didn't know what to make of it.

The nervous flutters remained the rest of the weekend as I waited for him to test the waters one more time, but that was the last of the jokes. When it came time to head home on the third day, the boys waited in the car while I gave my final hugs. I received what seemed like an especially long, tight squeeze from Dad. I wondered if I was imagining it until I looked up into his eyes and saw pride looking back into mine.

Traffic was light as I traveled up I-75 toward Atlanta. Clouds were scattered across the sky, shielding me from the harsh brightness of the sun. The boys were once again staring contentedly at their phones, completely ignoring me or any of our surroundings. I turned off the music, eager for the peace that comes from the meditative sound of the tires thrumming on the road.

It wasn't long before the Nudge spoke up. It turned out she didn't just give me directions for life, she also reminded me of what was true. "You're actually leaving your family without feeling ashamed of who you are."

I felt stunned by that statement. I thought back on all the times I'd spent with my family and realized she was right. I did often leave them feeling ashamed, like I had to work hard to make them proud of me. I felt into my body, seeking that familiar feeling of shame. It wasn't there.

That's when it dawned on me. The pride I saw in Dad's eyes was a reflection of the pride I already held for myself because I didn't need his validation anymore. I had embraced my own opinions and beliefs and risked vulnerably sharing them with him. I let myself be known by him for who I was, not who I thought he might prefer.

Oh my god, I thought. *I actually love myself.* I felt that truth spread out from my heart through my entire body before spilling out in big fat tears down my face. I said it again out loud, validating my own truth: "For the first time in my life that I remember, I can truly say I love myself."

This was a stunning turnabout from that moment in the kitchen years earlier, when I fell to the floor in disbelief of how much I hated myself. I looked around and noticed that the world shone brighter, the sound of my kids' laughter was sweeter, even the drivers around me seemed more considerate.

It was then I realized that while I was busy remembering who I was as a child, creating new boundaries, and standing up for myself, I'd been imperceptibly accepting the authentic me. In those moments, I'd been cultivating self-love. As I drove away from my family in Florida, I took a deep breath and smiled wide in recognition that that was what it felt like to love myself up close.

It was a moment I was grateful was imprinted on my brain because I would need to return to it often as doubt crept back in. After almost forty years of not loving myself, self-love was going to be a practice I would need to actively cultivate.

Chapter Twenty Two

During the pandemic, while I was reacquainting myself with the natural world, I undertook two certifications to learn how to use energy to heal animals (including humans). These certifications—Healing Touch for Animals and Animal Energy—not only deepened my ability to communicate with nature but also built upon what I'd learned in nature-based coach training. I wanted to use my new tools to encourage others to build their own relationship with nature.

The interesting thing was that these trainings showed me how disconnected I still was from most of humanity. I loved how connected I'd become with myself and the small group of women in the Coven, but those safe connections made me want to remain tight in the bud, not blossom like I was made for.

I felt uncomfortable and awkward out in the world. I wished I had a manual on how to be human, one that showed me the rules everyone else seemed to innately know so I could find a way to be happy within the confines of whatever structure they were following.

At one point, I'd thought I knew the rules. I'd done all the things I was told would make a good life: got married, had kids, bought a house in the suburbs. I volunteered when I could. I went to church. I exercised and ate healthy. I thought I'd get bonus points for healing myself of multiple sclerosis and hugging strangers, but none of it led to sustained happiness.

I was introduced to life coach Susan Hyatt in 2018. She was bold, audacious, and confronting—everything I'd been told I couldn't be. I admired her and I wanted to emulate her. She was the closest I'd found to someone living a human experience I'd be happy with. In the Spring of 2023, I signed up for her Bare coaching certification class. I hoped it was the manual I'd been seeking. I wanted to continue to love myself not only when I was by myself but also out in the world, where I continued to compare myself to others who seemed to have it all together. Out in the world, I continued to wonder where I belonged.

The first time I went to one of Susan's in-person events was her annual Yes Bash weekend retreat that June. The theme of Friday night's party was Main Character Energy. We were invited to wear something that made us feel like the main character in our own lives, an outfit that took us out of our supporting roles and into the one we were created for.

By the time I arrived at my Airbnb in Susan's hometown of Evansville, Indiana, I already suspected the weekend would be like none I'd ever experienced. I climbed the stairs to my second floor loft less than a half-mile from the Ohio river. I couldn't see it from my balcony, but I felt the power of it in my bones.

I stepped through the kitchen and entered the bed-room through a door to the left of the stove. The bed was adorned with an oversized fluffy blanket and soft, inviting pillows. I wanted to flop onto the bed, curl up into a ball, and sleep, but I wasn't there to remain tight in a bud. I was there to push through the discomfort of blossoming.

I dropped my laptop bag by the desk and brought my suitcase to the walk-in closet, where I hung up my numerous outfits. I still hadn't decided which one made me feel most like the main character of my life. Once I put everything away, I began my own fashion montage à la every romantic comedy ever made.

There was no full-size mirror in the loft, so I used my phone to take video in the kitchen. where I found the most flattering light. The first outfit I tried on was a tight green business dress. I strutted my stuff for the camera. I looked good, the color was phenomenal, and it had a sexy cutout at the center of my chest. But I felt like I'd be tug-ging at the skirt the whole night, trying to smooth out the creases caused by the dress bunching up over my ample hips. Not main character energy.

Next, I sashayed down my makeshift catwalk in a pair of soft, linen pants with a simple tank top. Boring. It was the epitome of supporting character energy.

Finally, I posed in the outfit I wanted to wear but wasn't sure I had the courage. The straight-leg sequin pants were silver and fit me like a glove. The top was a white, strappy crop top with a crocheted overlay. There was just enough skin between the top and the pants to be sexy but subtle.

Doubt crept in. Was I showing too much skin? Was I thin enough to get away with something like this? Would my fat rolls make an appearance and give me a muffin top? I was contemplating all these questions as I walked toward my phone to review the footage it'd captured.

I pressed play. Goddamn, I looked good. Was it okay for me to think that?

I imagined what Susan Hyatt would say, the queen of anti-dieting and fierce advocate for audacious self-acceptance. She'd say, "Hell, yeah, you look like a million bucks! Let the haters hate." Or something along those lines.

I did look damn good. The outfit was absolutely the epitome of my main character energy—a little sparkle, a little skin, and a whole lot of sass. I wanted desperately to be brave enough to claim it. The only way I knew how was to just show up and do it. I left the outfit on and went into the bathroom to finish getting ready. When my hair was half-up in a bejeweled hair clip and my eyes were subtly smoky, I finished the look with a nude lip and walked back down the steps of my Airbnb, feeling bold and ready to claim my main character energy even as my knees shook.

Susan rented an entire restaurant for the hundred or so women she was hosting for the weekend. I pulled into my parking spot, checked my makeup in the rearview mirror, took a deep breath, and walked toward the front door. A few other women in their own bold outfits, looking better than me, were walking in as I arrived. I walked through the door behind them, feeling my confidence wane a little.

Once I'd finished checking in with Megan, Susan's assistant, I looked around just in time to see two gorgeous drag queens and a drag king walk by. This was definitely turning into my kind of party. I got swept up in the sea of women introducing themselves to me and launching into excited chatter about the weekend. I allowed myself to fully receive their compliments about my outfit. I stood up straighter and held my head higher.

With each compliment, I felt more courageous about owning my place at that party. I confidently introduced myself to people whose faces I recognized but had never met. When the platform that was taking 360-degree selfies became available, I jumped at the chance to be in the spotlight.

The women at that party behaved in ways I'd never seen before. They were confident, encouraging, bold, loud, full of wonder and joy. They ordered burgers and fries and ate everything on their plates. They were curious and interested. They were full of life, and their positive energy was contagious. Despite the fact that my lifestyle probably didn't match up with most of theirs, I felt like I belonged. I went to bed that evening with a full belly and an overflowing heart.

The next morning, I rose early to walk to the conference room where the next day's festivities were held. One of the first to arrive, I was mesmerized by the gorgeous, feminine decorations.

Megan approached to get me checked in once again. "Welcome! Did you bring your name tag?"

Shit. We were asked to bring them, and in my haste to get out that morning, I forgot. "I don't have it, but you can write my name on my arm." I boldly suggested, still feeling brazen after the previous night's party.

She was appalled and refused to write in permanent marker on my arm.

"No, really, I want you to," I said, but she just wouldn't do it.

Not to be deterred, I found someone willing: Susan's husband Scott, who I'd briefly met the night before. After securing a permanent marker from Megan's stash, I approached him while other women were beginning to file in. "Hey Scott! I met you last night. It's great to see you. Would you mind writing my name on my arm? I forgot my name badge."

He hesitantly agreed. I held out my right arm and pointed to just below the edge of my t-shirt. "Write, 'my name is' across my arm, then write 'Melinda' down my arm, please."

Once my "name tag" was in place, I flowed freely around the room, taking in the stunning floral centerpieces on each table, the brightly colored balloon arch surrounding the stage that held what I later learned was the "crying couch," and the elaborate gifts waiting at each seat. Eventually I made my way over to the tables on the other side of the room. More gifts waited to be claimed by each participant, along with coffee and tea service to start the day. After pouring hot water into a delicate teacup, I chose a vibrant black tea to steep and added a cube of sugar infused with rose petals. I brought the tea to a table at the back of the room already filled with a few other women from the Bare coach training.

My outfit was a stark contrast to the previous evening's sparkle pants. I wore a gray t-shirt with LOVE printed across the chest, tucked into comfortable black pants. I thought I'd feel stylishly casual. Instead, I felt frumpy amidst the sea of color everyone else was wearing. I felt a hit to my confidence but was still riding so high from the evening before I thought I'd be able to weather it and own my comfort.

We spent the day listening to Susan speak and coach volunteers on the couch that lived up to its name. Listening to one of the participants sharing her story, I began to quietly weep. It's not so much that I resonated with her story but that listening to it brought up the feelings of unworthiness and shame that still lingered. The judgmental thoughts began again. *Who was I to think that I belonged among these successful, inspiring women? What had I done that was even remotely as impressive as what they've accomplished?* The shame drowned out the voice of self-love I discovered after visiting my dad in Florida.

I started to believe I was fooling myself to think I belonged among these women. I didn't hear anything else that was said before the next quick break was announced. I remained at the table, tried to make myself as invisible as possible, and continued to quietly cry.

Kristine, who was taking the Bare coach training with me, noticed my tears and sat in the empty seat next to me. She leaned in and gently asked, "Hey, honey. What's wrong?"

I shook my head, unwilling to dump my shame in her lap.

Refusing to be dismissed, she tried again. "What's bringing on these tears?"

I lifted my head just enough to peek at her. There was no pity on her face, only concern and curiosity. "I just have feelings of unworthiness coming up, even though last night was the first time I really felt like I belonged," I said.

"Of course you belong, Melinda," Kristine said. "But I get it. Sometimes that unworthiness can tear us down. Do you mind if I help you unpack some of this?" She was asking for permission to coach me. After agreeing to her generous offer, I heard her affirm for me: "Only you get to decide your own worth."

My story of unworthiness felt sticky, like the remnants of glue left on a window from a sticker that had spent years in place. It was going to take the right tools with the right type of solution to dissolve it completely.

Kristine validated my experience with her own stories of unworthiness, which helped me feel seen and less alone. It removed some of the glue stuck from my story, but there was still enough left that it kept me in shame the rest of the weekend despite my attempts to overcome it with a "fake it till you make it" attitude. That wasn't the right tool or solution.

* * *

I wondered if celebrating myself with a photoshoot for my forty-eighth birthday could be the solution I needed to dissolve the shame. I felt courageous and curious enough to try.

Shortly after making this decision, I was mindlessly scrolling through Instagram when I came across a post from Jade Beall. I'd admired her work for years. Her unretouched photographs of nude bodies of all shapes and sizes looked like works of art.

Leaning against the edge of my comfort zone, I decided to take my chances and reach out to her. Based on her level of talent, I expected her prices to be well outside my budget. When she promptly returned my email with the details and prices of her photo shoots, I was floored. Not only would I be able to book my own nude photo shoot but I also had enough in my budget to book an extra day or two in Arizona, where she was based.

That's how I found myself flying out to Tucson in August, the day before I turned forty-eight. In the months leading up to the trip, I continued to practice feeling worthy, but the glue was stubborn.

When the Lyft driver in Tucson pulled off the highway and began winding their way through a neighborhood of homes with chain link fences and "Beware of Dog" signs, I wondered what I'd gotten myself into. I'd been looking forward to staying in luxury at the Tuxon, but after pulling through the large gate protecting the hotel like a fortress, it looked more like a Motel 8 than the updated hotel I'd seen on the Booking.com app. I wanted to leave immediately and find a new hotel, but it seemed as though we were in the middle of nowhere, and I didn't have any other options.

It was still hours until check-in, so I ordered myself a beer and nachos at the bar, then sat down at a table to see what else I could find. About halfway through my beer, I still hadn't found a better place to stay, so I took a break and finally looked at my surroundings. The lounge area was clean and inviting. There was a coffee stand to my left that looked like it was available all day. A large sign was propped up next to the bar announcing a corporate event that would be taking place later that day.

Through the wall of windows in front of me was a pool with a few people lounging around. Large plants surrounded the pool, creating a lush, tropical feel. There were gorgeous flowers hanging from pots, bringing life to another outdoor seating area. I looked again at the bar with its polished wood and tall, elegant barstools. I was beginning to wonder if I'd been too hasty in my judgment of the hotel.

After I finished off the plate of nachos, I found my room was ready. I grabbed my bags and a second beer and followed a staff member through a door at the back of the lounge. He led me up a flight of stairs along the outside of the hotel. We turned a corner, and I sucked in my breath at the unexpected beauty of a small mountain directly in front of us. I decided I was glad I'd stayed.

He showed me to my room, then left as soon as I unlocked my door. The room was stunning. The artwork on the walls reflected the unconventional beauty right outside my door. The fixtures were modern and sleek. Even the movable partition that closed off the bathroom for privacy in this open-concept room was a work of art. It wasn't the luxury I'd imagined, but it was a luxury that suited me even better.

That evening, I donned my bright orange one-piece suit, grabbed the latest Stephen King novel, and headed for the pool. Hugs were the last thing on my mind as I lay out my towel on a lounge chair.

After a third beer with dinner, I had some liquid courage to approach another solo traveler cooling off in the pool. Her name was Lucy, and we became so engrossed in our conversation that we didn't even notice the large corporate event happening inside, just beyond the wall of windows.

Lucy was intrigued by my reason for being in Tucson and offered to take photos of me in my bathing suit to prep for the next day. I mustered up the confidence of my main character energy and posed, feeling incredibly vulnerable and ridiculous. She directed me to adopt poses that were far outside my comfort zone, but somehow she made them work. Despite the awkwardness of both of us being half-naked, I leaned in for a grateful hug.

"You're the most interesting person I've ever met," Lucy said.

This ground everything to a halt. In that one statement, she revealed that the sticky glue from my unworthiness story was still very present. For the rest of our conversation, I was distracted by my brain continuing to chew on what she'd said. I knew she regularly interacted with doctors and high-profile people in her line of work. What could I have done or said that was more interesting than they were? When I finally fell asleep that evening, I still didn't have an answer.

I wasn't meeting Jade for the sunset photo shoot until early evening, so I spent the day discovering Tucson and pampering myself with a mani/pedi. When it was time for the shoot, Jade picked me up from the hotel and drove us out to the first location in the desert.

Along the way, Jade soothed my nerves by explaining that I could wear or not wear whatever I wanted. She said I was in control of the evening, and she was just there to capture my divinity. She even called her shoots photo "ceremonies" to honor the sacredness of the moments she captured with her lens.

After my nerves settled some, we talked about our shared love of humanity and our desire for more connection in the world. We were kindred spirits. The time we spent connecting in her van on the way to the desert allowed me to truly feel safe and ready to be vulnerable in her presence.

The stunning saguaro cacti grew in stature as we wound our way up a mountain toward her preferred location. When Jade parked her van, I felt my nerves rise again. "Jade? Will people be walking by while we're shooting?"

"There shouldn't be too many people," she said. "Besides, the trails are pretty far from where we'll be."

That gave my brain something else to freak out about. "So we won't be taking a trail to get to where we're going? Do I need to watch out for snakes and scorpions?"

"Oh honey," she said, "we'll be all right. I'll be on the lookout. I know what to look for. In all the years I've been doing this, no one has ever been bit or stung."

"Um, okay." I decided to trust that she had me.

Once we got to the site, Jade noticed storm clouds developing in the distance. "The light is gorgeous right now but we'll have to shoot pretty quick because that storm may be making its way to us."

I removed my pants, but left my shirt and underwear on. "Can we start like this?" I asked. The shirt was maroon, off the shoulder, and read "Rebel Girl" across the chest. My underwear was a sexy, satin, full-bottom leopard print. The shirt/underwear combo felt more sensual to me than being fully nude, although I knew those would come later.

"Honey, this is your shoot. You can wear whatever you want."

Over the next hour and a half, Jade shot me in all states of dress and undress, even with a tiara at times. I heard her shout from a distance, "Yes, queen! You are gorgeous! All your ancestors are cheering you on and celebrating you for the glorious beauty you are. The cacti are reveling in your beauty and accentuating all that you are. They want you dancing with them!"

I felt my arms and heart grow wider as I flowed with the music in my head. I was completely at ease even without a stitch of clothing. As Jade moved me from one position to another, I noticed the storm clouds becoming more menacing. Lightning streaked across the sky. "Oh my god!" I said. "Please tell me you're getting shots of that storm behind me."

"Oh, I'm trying," Jade replied. "Stand right there next to the saguaro. You'll be in perfect position."

I felt the universe conspiring with me. I drew power up from the dry stillness of the earth and down from the crackling electricity shooting across the sky. I felt fierce, like the warrior I knew my ancestors believed me to be. I moved with the inspiration, never once questioning my worthiness or where I belonged in the world. I belonged right there, to the earth, to the sky, to my ancestors, to myself. I roared, posed, danced, and just let myself go.

When the storm finally drew closer, we made a mad dash for the van, reaching it at the same time the first few drops of rain fell.

"That was exhilarating!" I exclaimed.

"I've never had a photo ceremony like that before," Jade said. "That was absolutely incredible. I'm pretty sure I got a few shots of the lightning as well." And she had. A few weeks later, she sent me powerful images that looked like I was wearing the glow from the lightning as a halo.

We were still only halfway through the shoot. Next, we drove away from the natural environment and toward the intimacy of a private studio located in a teepee in Jade's backyard.

Before starting up again, she invited me in to her home. In the kitchen, her shelves displayed clear jars filled with nuts and spices. "What's this one?" I asked, pointing to a jar with what looked like berries but unlike any I'd ever seen.

"Oh, that's saguaro fruit," she said. "It's only possible to harvest once a year, and it's so difficult it's not worth selling on the market. So the only way to get them is to harvest them yourself, which I do painstakingly every year. Would you like to try one?"

I felt guilty for taking one after hearing what she went through to get them, but I desperately wanted to try it. Despite shame trying to take hold, I was determined to continue doing things differently. I was determined to believe in my worthiness. I felt deep discomfort in my body as I nodded yes and accepted the fruit.

It was unlike anything I'd ever tasted before. It was about the size and shape of a mulberry, but covered in little seeds that popped as I bit down. I don't even know how to describe the flavor except that it tasted like earthy nourishment. I felt honored and humbled that Jade shared this sacred fruit with me.

After replenishing ourselves with the saguaro fruit and water, we finished out the next ninety minutes in the comfort of her studio, where I danced along to P!nk and once again rocked my silver sequined pants in front of the camera. Jade dropped me back off at my hotel that night, where I slept deeply in gratitude for the greatest gift I'd ever given myself.

* * *

By the time I joined Susan Hyatt's next retreat two months later in Savannah, Georgia, the question of whether or not I belonged no longer existed. I finally knew deep down in my bones that I had always belonged, just not to any place outside myself. I'd always belonged to me.

I still had a long way to go in breaking old habits and patterns of unworthiness with others. I'd practiced them for so long, the wound ran deep. I knew that believing in my self-worth wouldn't happen overnight, but based on the experiences I had with Jade and the women I met through Susan Hyatt's community, I was able to whole-heartedly believe that the supportive relationships I'd witnessed on the cross-country trip were not only possible for me, but inevitable.

Chapter Twenty Three

To choose to love others up close means choosing to be a witness to their pain and suffering. I could only know another as much as I was willing to be open to the validity of their experience, no matter what I believed. Where did that leave me when their experience caused me pain and suffering?

As a child, I felt the suffering of the world deeply. I'd tearfully ask my parents, "Why are people so mean?" They could never give me a satisfying answer.

"Why does there have to be so much suffering? How could God allow so much pain in the world?" I'd try again, thinking maybe they'd have a better answer to one of those questions. They didn't.

I noticed that my entire family, including cousins, grandparents, aunts, and uncles, ignored the suffering of the world when we were together. I didn't blame them. We got together so infrequently, it was understandable nobody wanted to ruin the fun. But as a child, I was looking for someone who shared my big feelings. I didn't understand why I had them or what I was supposed to do with them.

Instead all my feelings seemed to do was make the people around me uncomfortable. They reminded me that I was too sensitive for my own good and left me believing I was powerless. I couldn't even rely on the power of my anger because without guidance on what to do with it, it became explosive, misdirected, and bullying.

The only times I actually felt powerful was when I was in control—control of my emotions, control of my surroundings, and control of my experiences. But control was an illusion. It was a false sense of power, one that teetered on a scale of judgments. One word of doubt sent it crashing down, just as one word of approval weighted it to the other side. Everything in my life relied on the opinions and validation of others, and no amount of control could help me maintain a consistent balance of power out in the world.

When I drove back from Florida full of the knowledge that I truly loved myself again, I recognized that the practice and work I'd been doing ever since my early morning adult tantrum was slowly laying a new foundation built on authenticity, self-love, self-acceptance, self-reliance, true connections, and strength of character. I knew who I was and I really liked her. It felt good to say that not only did I love me but also I really liked me.

With this new foundation, I vowed to never again crumble from the weight of others' judgments. I knew the pain of rejection, abandonment, and disapproval would still hurt—my big feelings told me so. But never again would I reject, abandon, or disapprove of myself. I knew that no matter what, I belonged to me, and any connections I made were just icing on the cake. The relationships I lost might have caused me to grieve, but they didn't deplete my worth.

Knowing something and putting it into practice, however, are two very different things.

In early 2024, I began working for someone who I considered a friend. We'd met when I was scouting farms for a Healing Touch for Animals level 1 class in Atlanta.

"Do you think the barn will be cool enough if the weather's especially hot the day of class? October can be pretty unpredictable," I said to Nicole as we toured her farm.

"Everything's figureoutable," she responded.

I smiled over at her. "Marie Forleo?" I asked, assuming that's whose book she got the message from.

She smiled at me and nodded, our connection officially forged. That class never came to be, but it wasn't the last I heard from her. I got to do energy work on some of her horses and sometimes she'd sign up for my workshops.

During one particular workshop, we remained on the video call after everyone else left. She updated me on the status of her relationship and lamented that she couldn't find a consistent, reliable person to help her with work around the barn.

"You could hire me," I suggested.

She didn't take my suggestion seriously at first so I tried again. "What do you need help with at the barn?" I asked.

"Mucking stalls and some general cleaning and up-keep of the property."

"This is going to sound crazy," I said, "but mucking stalls is one of my favorite things to do. I find it meditative and fulfilling. I'd love to help."

"Really?" She seemed surprised. "I've had eight people out to the barn already, and none of them have worked out. One didn't even bother collecting her pay after training for a day."

"If I don't think it's a good fit, I'll let you know," I said. "I'm in need of a little extra income right now, and this would be an ideal solution for me."

"Can you come out to the farm this weekend?" she asked.

I responded with a resounding yes and agreed to meet her for the first training that next Sunday.

My heart swelled as soon as I stepped foot in the barn. The horses were already out in the pasture, but I relished the smell of hay mixed with the musky scent the horses left behind. I shadowed Nicole as she showed me the very precise way she preferred to have her stalls cleaned. "I know I'm giving you a lot of detail, but I've spent years honing what works and what doesn't. The system I have in place is the most efficient and keeps the barn as clean as possible," she explained.

"Sounds good," I said. "I prefer being given detailed instructions so I can be sure I'm doing my job well."

Not only would I be getting the extra income I needed but I'd also basically be getting paid to exercise and spend time with horses. It was a dream. Even though the farm was almost an hour away, I looked forward to using the travel time for reflection and meditation.

When I arrived that first day after training, I grabbed my tools and began mucking the first stall. What took Nicole ten minutes took me forty-five. I looked around, wondering what I'd done so differently from her that it took that much longer. I did some calculations in my head and realized it was going to take six hours to finish all eight stalls. I wasn't prepared for that. Overwhelm filled my head with pressure.

At that moment, Nicole came to check on me. "Hey, I'm going to get started on some of these other stalls while you get used to mucking, okay?"

I took a deep breath of relief once I found out I wasn't expected to do it all right away, then moved on to the next stall.

One week later, I arrived at the farm and Nicole still hadn't brought the horses out to pasture. I took my time connecting with each one, stroking their soft velvet noses if they let me. I was in heaven. When Nicole finally came to lead them out to the pastures, I grabbed a large pitch-fork and began mucking the first stall.

Not wanting to disappoint Nicole, I spent extra time that morning trying to perfect my mucking skills, but it wasn't working. In fact, it was taking me far longer than usual, and it almost felt like the mess was multiplying. I was so confused. I didn't know why it felt so hard that morning when I'd really gotten the hang of it by the end of the previous week. The overwhelm returned.

After leading all the horses out to the pastures, Nicole walked over to me. "How's it going?" she asked.

"I don't know," I said. "I don't seem to have a handle on it today and I don't know why. It doesn't make any sense."

"Have you tried moving from one end of the stall to the other in a pattern?" she asked, sharing a tip she'd already given me multiple times.

"Yes, but I—"

She cut me off, continuing to offer suggestions that were really just more of the exact same details she'd already given me. It wasn't helpful.

"Do you ever just have days when you're off?" I asked, knowing that was probably all it was.

"Yeah, but this isn't difficult work," she said, adding shame to the frustration I was already feeling.

"Okay, thanks." I waited until she walked away, then broke down crying. I felt so stupid. So childish. I didn't understand why I was having such a hard time. I was embarrassed to be seen as so incompetent in front of her. It took a minute, but when I realized that the shame I felt was mine and didn't actually come from her, I gave myself grace and her the benefit of the doubt. I decided she wasn't judging me, just trying to encourage me the best way she knew how.

Most days, I was left alone to do my work except when it was time to teach me new responsibilities. I picked everything up pretty easily, but occasionally I asked clarifying questions because it helped me do a better job when I understood why I was doing what I was doing.

Nicole often cut off those questions, curtly repeating what she'd already said and reinforcing what I needed to do without addressing why. When I tried telling her that it helped me to know why tasks were done the way they were, she dismissed me and continued to train me in the same inflexible, abrupt way. I learned to just stop asking.

Eventually I noticed a similar pattern in our other interactions. In the midst of me sharing a personal story about my life, Nicole cut me off, shared a story of her own that I'd heard many times before, and walked away without giving me the opportunity to finish my own story.

Eventually I stopped speaking to her altogether. I showed up, got my work done, enjoyed the horses, and left.

Over time, a few of the horses were moved to a different farm, leaving only five stalls left to clean. Five stalls didn't provide me enough income to justify the two-hour round trip to the farm and back. Nicole agreed to give me the added responsibility of feeding the horses and leading them to pasture to make up for the lost income. I was thrilled at the prospect of working directly with them but also terrified because I'd never handled horses before. Even when I did energy work, the owner was always there to maintain control of the horse. They're enormous creatures capable of great harm if you don't know what you're doing.

Nicole listened to my fears and assured me that she'd give me plenty of training. And after four training sessions, I did finally feel comfortable enough to bring the horses out to the pastures by myself while Nicole watched from the sidelines. Soon I'd be doing it all on my own. I felt ready.

With over thirty years of horse experience, Nicole took the horses out two or three at a time. I wanted to work my way up to being comfortable with that because it'd make me more efficient and also alleviate the stress on the horses who didn't like being separated even temporarily. I figured that after a few months' time, I'd be ready.

Instead it was less than a week later that Nicole asked if I was ready to bring out two horses together. I felt stunned. I'd just gotten comfortable with bringing them out one by one. "No, I'm not ready to do that today," I said, imagining the danger I might place myself in if I didn't lead the horses into the pasture properly. I was afraid I'd somehow get their leads crossed or, even worse, we'd come across a snake or something else that spooked them. I barely knew how to corral one horse when things went sideways, I couldn't imagine being ready to corral two at the same time.

"Well, today is the perfect day," Nicole said. "My two horses are the calmest horses you'll ever come across, and the gate is already open, so you won't have to worry about that."

"I understand, but I'm not ready today," I reiterated. I couldn't understand why she was pushing me when I'd already voiced my fears and she'd assured me she'd give me all the training I needed.

"What more do you think you need to be ready?" she questioned harshly.

"More time and experience," I said. "I want to know I can manage the horses when the unexpected arises."

"The only way you're going to get comfortable is by doing it," she continued to push. "And today is the perfect day."

"But I can't make myself be ready just because the conditions are best for learning," I said, beginning to cry. I was feeling my frustrations from all the other times she hadn't listened to me rise to the surface.

"I don't know how much more training I can offer you, Melinda. Most people only need three to five lessons, you're already at seven."

I felt the shame race red-hot through my body, which made me cry even harder. "I understand, and if you can't keep training me, let me know and you can find someone else for this position," I said. "But you asked if I could lead two horses to the field, and I'm telling you I'm not ready."

I refused to put myself in a position I wasn't ready for, especially in that emotional state. Nicole just continued to argue that I should lead the two horses together. Finally, in a fit of frustration and confusion, I said, "You don't listen to me. You asked me if I could do it, and I said no. This is not the first time you haven't listened. I've gotten to the point where I don't even bother talking to you anymore."

"What do you mean you can't talk to me?" she asked, maintaining a cool, calm demeanor despite the rise in my voice and the waterfall of tears streaming down my face. "If you didn't think you could talk to me, you should have said something."

I was dumbfounded, not knowing what else to say. I prayed she'd fire me on the spot, but she kept trying to get me to lead both horses that day. I cried and argued, somehow unaware that I could be the one to quit, until thankfully one of the horse's owners showed up and disrupted our fight. Nicole walked away to greet the client, while I grabbed the tools I needed to muck stalls. I left the two horses for her to lead to the pasture.

I sobbed while mucking the stalls, letting the hard, physical labor move shame and anger through my body. I loved those horses and I loved that barn, but I wasn't sure I could continue working under those conditions. The thought of not returning filled me with deep grief.

Just before I finished mucking my first stall, Nicole walked over. "Melinda, are you listening to something?" she asked, noting the ear buds in my ears that I often wore for comfort without listening to anything.

I shook my head.

"I'm sorry," she said, and I felt my shoulders drop and relief flood my body. "It's just that I need you to understand . . ."

I didn't hear her finish. A whooshing sound pulsed through my ears in time with the quickening of my heart. This was no damn apology.

"Nicole, now is not the time to talk," I said. "I'm not capable of continuing a conversation with you right now."

"But I don't think it's fair that you didn't come to me when you had trouble talking to me," she persisted.

"I can't talk right now. Please just let me finish my work, and we'll talk another day," I muttered through gritted teeth. I blinked rapidly to keep my tears at bay.

Nicole kept at it, trying to talk to me while my big feelings threatened to spill over. I was afraid they would cause me to say something I'd regret, so I took a deep breath, closed my eyes, and slowly reiterated, "Today is not the day. I am having a meltdown and am not rationally thinking, so I can't continue this conversation with you."

"Just give me an example of a time when I didn't listen to you," she pushed.

"*Now! Right now*! I've told you I can't talk to you right now, but you keep trying. You are not listening right now!" I exploded.

Shockingly, it still took another few nonsensical back-and-forth arguments before she finally walked out. As soon as she was gone, I lost it. I sobbed while clinging to the mucking pitchfork for dear life. When I finally calmed enough, I finished the rest of the stalls, releasing pent-up energy through exertion.

The next few days left me in a state of shame that re-energized old habits of thought. *What did I do so wrong? Why was I so sensitive? That meltdown was childish. I really take things to the extreme. If I'd just been more of an adult, I probably could have brought those two horses to the field without incident. Why did I make such a big deal of it all? Why did I freak out so bad? I'm so ridiculous, overly sensitive, immature, dramatic.*

I didn't want to ever deal with Nicole again, but thinking about quitting left me feeling like a runaway child unwilling to face her problems. I wondered what other adult humans might do in my situation but had no answers. I wasn't scheduled to work again until the following weekend, so I spent the next few days praying for clarity.

On the morning of the third day, I felt the clouds part in my mind. I saw that I'd spent so much time allowing people to talk to me in shaming ways that I'd become accustomed to internalizing that shame as mine. I'd spent years excusing other people's behaviors while berating myself for my own.

But I knew too much now. I knew this wasn't the way kind, compassionate people spoke to one another. I knew this wasn't the kind of relationship I'd ever tolerate again.

My big feelings had known immediately what it took my mind three days to accept: Nicole was manipulating and coercing me. This didn't make her bad, it simply made her bad for me. I knew I needed to quit not because I was running away but because I was no longer willing to be treated that way.

I was hesitant to text her with my decision because I knew the backlash I'd receive. I was afraid my body would respond to that backlash with the same shame and confusion that had led to my meltdown in the first place. I barely had time to register that fear before I questioned it. What if the meltdown was a gift from my body to show me the injustice of what was happening? What if my big feelings had always been there to tell me what I needed to know?

This time, instead of fearing and judging those big feelings, I asked for their advice. They let me know without words they no longer wanted to work for Nicole. I agreed with them, but as soon as I acknowledged it, my body began to shake. The big feelings had something more to say. "The way she talks to us is not okay. We don't have to accept it," they told me.

I knew instantly what they meant and what I needed to do. Despite my brain thinking I was being immature and dramatic, I typed out a text to Nicole. "I've thought a lot about what happened the other day, and I've come to the conclusion that working on your farm is no longer the best fit for me. I will not be returning." I hit send, then blocked her number from my phone, her profiles from my socials, and her email from my safe sender list. My brain kept telling me I was overreacting, but my body felt free.

This was something I recognized when I was having my meltdown on the farm and the tantrum on my bed. It was a deep, familiar sense that my body knew something different than my mind believed. It was the same sense I had every time the Nudge spoke to me. The Nudge and my big feelings were the intelligence of my body, a vastly superior intelligence than my mind for making decisions about my life.

I ignored my body for so long because she deviated from the rules of culture. She asked me to do things that didn't make sense in the "real" world. She asked me to make choices that others might deem selfish, extreme, naive. But she always knew better. When I listened to her guidance, I felt empowered and fulfilled regardless of the outcome. When I followed culture's strict rules, I felt completely powerless.

I began wondering if it was possible that she not only knew what I needed, but also what was to come? Was it possible she was tapped into the collective consciousness?

When the Nudge, a part of my body's intelligence, suggested going on each of my hug journeys, there was an immediacy to her message. She made me feel like it was my choice to do them or not—but if I was going to do them, they needed to happen right away.

Did she send me on MYOH to witness the beauty and love of a thousand strangers so I didn't completely lose faith when, less than a year later, Sandy Hook would take place?

Did she send me on the cross-country trip to be filled with the kindness and connection of people across the country because she knew just months later all of humanity would be placed in a time-out?

Whatever it was, I'm grateful to that body intelligence in the form of both the Nudge and my big feelings. They no longer have to be so loud. I feel them whisper in the morning before dawn, inviting me on a walk. I feel them smile when I'm holding just the right peach to buy. I feel them fill me with energy just before choosing the right kind of hard.

And I know they'll always be there, just like they were when I was five years old at the church fair. Letting me know before my name was called that the gold purse was already mine.

Chapter Twenty Four

Loving someone up close is hard. It's messy, complicated, and unbelievably, stunningly beautiful.

When I set out to hug strangers in 2011, I believed I knew what it was to love another. I thought it was unconditional, and that as long as I stayed out of judgment, I could love people despite the choices they made or the people they hurt—even if that person was me. What I didn't know was that loving them unconditionally would take more than staying out of judgment. It would take vulnerability, extreme self-love, and boundaries.

Most of my life, I presented a pretty version of myself to others. Because of this, I had trouble holding authentic relationships. When I first risked removing the pretty mask and sharing a truer, rawer version of myself, I thought I was going to die. Literally. I got short of breath, my heart raced, and I felt like I was going to pass out.

When I didn't die—and, even more surprisingly, that version of me was accepted—I risked it again. The next time was a little more bearable, but I still had to breathe deeply, willing myself not to pass out. Nowadays when I enter vulnerable territory, I still get weak knees and my voice shakes, but rather than feeling like I'm going to die, I actually feel fully alive.

During the pandemic, I discovered that I could actually develop relationships with people by phone or over Zoom that were as deep, if not deeper, than the ones I made with people I could physically hug when I leaned into that vulnerability.

When I hugged strangers, family, or friends without vulnerability, a distance remained. A distance that kept me from being truly known. A distance that at times was necessary, but that at other times kept me from building the kind of relationships I wanted.

The risk to be that vulnerable was terrifying, but the reward was getting to live the best version of myself out loud. It was knowing that the people who chose me did so because they loved all of me up close. This validation empowered me to believe I'm worthy because no one else on Earth can be a better version of Melinda than I can.

I wasn't able to know extreme self-love until I risked being vulnerable with myself. Through these hug journeys, I discovered that I was denying and abandoning the parts of myself I loved the least. In doing so, I'd lost the best of myself, the most sensitive aspects. They were my truest, rawest parts.

When MYOH ended, I was confused. I didn't know who I was anymore because love didn't look like I thought it would. It asked so much more of me than I was willing to give—until I took the blinders off and saw that in denying my best parts, I was denying the best parts of the people I loved too. The parts we were all afraid to show to the world because we feared rejection and abandonment.

Connection and belonging are a core need to survive in this world. Most of us would rather abandon ourselves than risk being authentic in a world that simultaneously tells us to be ourselves but then shames us when we are.

I spent a lifetime abandoning myself for the sake of fitting in. I hid the parts that I was denying behind a carefully cultivated mask. Every time some authentic part of me was ridiculed, harshly judged, or flat-out ignored, I adjusted that mask. I thought I could continue to be me while presenting an acceptable self to the world.

The girl with the mask smiled prettily, emoting a sense of joy she didn't always feel. The girl with the mask learned all the right things to say in nearly all situations. And when she didn't know what to say, she knew to stay quiet. She knew what clothes to wear to hide her insecurities. She practiced applying just enough makeup so she didn't look so tired but not so much that she couldn't remain invisible if she wanted.

She always showed up early to a party so she could make friends with the host's pets while downing her first glass of wine to ease her way into socializing. She'd often wake the next morning in deep shame, afraid that the courage she found in that bottle of wine caused her to reveal too much of her truer, rawer self—a self she remained confused by.

By the time the cross-country hug trip ended, I was no longer confused about who I was, but I realized I no longer knew her. The mask had replaced all that she once was. I was soul-crushingly tired from carrying that mask around and had no choice but to rely on what I'd discovered about vulnerability to give me the courage to let it go, little by little, so I could know myself again.

I started dropping the mask in the comfort and safety of my home when the kids were with their dad. As I let it go, I wasn't sure if I was being authentic or if I was just doing the opposite of what I'd been conditioned to do. That's when I realized I couldn't do it alone. I needed witnesses to reflect my truth back to me. I had to drop my mask in front of the people with whom I felt safest.

I slowly revealed a more authentic version of myself to my family and closest friends. I felt seen and heard by them as they celebrated this truer version of me. I felt supported by them when they questioned something that felt forced, that didn't seem to align with the me they were getting to know. Through their eyes, I discovered the truest, rawest version of myself.

Some people say you have to love yourself first before you can love others. It seems more accurate to say that you have to be brave enough to believe in the possibility of your own worth before you can step into vulnerability with those you love. In that space, we learn to fully know ourselves while being accepted by the people who see the rawest versions of us and choose to continue loving us anyway. The more I was loved by others in my rawest form, the more deeply I got to know and fall in love with myself.

Leaning into that authenticity is a practice. The more my self-love grew, the more courage I had to reveal myself in other spaces until I found the strength to remain in my authenticity even when it was judged or denied. It was at that point that the mask stopped being who I was and became a tool I could use in new or uncomfortable spaces.

The world doesn't celebrate authenticity unless it conforms to the needs of the social hierarchies set in place. We must choose to celebrate our own authenticity instead. When we do, we give others permission to do the same. The more authentic I was with the people I love, the more authentic they were with me. We now get to be our weird selves together, and that is the greatest celebration I could ask for.

When I saw the promise of relationships built on authenticity, support, and trust during the cross-country trip, I knew I wouldn't settle for anything less. I was willing to surrender to the fear that cautioned me against removing my mask and bravely sought out relationships that reflected the type of love and acceptance I now believed I was worth.

That's when the hard work really began because loving people up close requires looking at that love daily and actively choosing it over and over again. It also requires the recognition of when the best way to love them is from a distance.

I once thought loving and being loved unconditionally literally meant without condition. I was wrong. As humans, we can't have unconditional love without boundaries. I tried so hard to love others unconditionally without boundaries, and it left me feeling powerless and angry. I began to resent the people who crossed boundaries I hadn't yet expressed.

Initially, I thought boundaries meant saying no when I didn't want to join the PTA. I thought they meant being selective about who I spent my time with. I thought they meant not letting people talk to my kids in ways that weren't acceptable. Those are all valid boundaries, and I was great at those, but they weren't enough.

The wounding I had around being abandoned by friends I thought loved me tried to stop me from creating the boundaries my body needed. It used reason and logic to tell me why my boundaries didn't make sense, why they were too much. To deny the possibility that I needed them in the first place.

Determined to reclaim my power in all areas of my life, I wondered if the wounding was wrong. I turned to my body intelligence for the answers. I let my big feelings guide me.

When I got angry at my ex-husband for once again requesting information about the kids' school that he had every ability to access for himself, I knew my anger was asking for a boundary to protect my mental energy.

When I got frustrated at my neighbor for offering unsolicited advice, I knew my frustration was asking me to place boundaries around how much of myself to share with others until they were proven trustworthy.

When I felt resentful toward the universe for not delivering to me the same things as the people I watched on social media, I knew my resentment was asking me to establish boundaries around the media I was consuming.

When I felt confused, weak, and aggrieved at Nicole's farm, I learned that my big feelings were asking me to establish boundaries around how I was willing to be treated.

As I established each new boundary, I discovered that it's a practice. It isn't always clear where the boundary is. Sometimes I asked for a boundary only to find out it was needed somewhere else or that it needed to be bigger, broader, or clearer. I continued and will continue to make lots of mistakes. This, too, is a gift of vulnerability because forgiveness is a salve that binds people even closer.

Ultimately I lost relationships, but they were ones that would have meant keeping the loose boundaries they were used to. They were relationships that kept me powerless. I learned I could only love those people unconditionally from a distance, so I let them go.

The ones who did accept my boundaries continue to accept them to this day. I love them unconditionally within the framework of my boundaries, while also receiving love from them within the framework of their own. We've learned to love each other up close.

There was a time when it felt too hard to be human. It was too confusing, messy, and dangerous. I wanted that to change, and I thought love was the answer. I thought sharing hugs with others was the solution to contributing more love to the world, and that if I could only do so enough, the world would become a kinder, gentler place in which to live.

The hugs showed me how little I knew of love. They showed me how much more confusing it is. The hugs simultaneously allowed me to see the kind, gentle world I believed in while also highlighting the messy, dangerous parts of humanity I wanted to run from.

It took time for me to understand that the hugs were highlighting those messy, dangerous parts of humanity as an invitation to understand them better. So I could understand myself better.

I see now that all the places where I denied my own humanity were the places where deeper love was waiting for me. In accepting it all, I learned that unconditional love is a verb, an action we take to allow for the greatest authentic expression of ourselves and all of humanity.

Why hugs? Because it's a simple expression for the very complicated thing we call love. After hugging a thousand strangers in 2011, I wasn't sure I ever wanted to hug a stranger again. But love called me forward. It asked me to embrace my big feelings and accept all of the messiness of humanity. It asked me to believe in the power of healed relationships. It asked me to dig deeper and learn how to love everyone to the best of my ability whether it's up close or at a distance. From this empowered place, I look forward to continuing to offer this physical expression of love to as many people as I can.

And, as I rest my hand tenderly on my chest, holding my own body with compassion and grace, I finally get it. The greatest, most meaningful hug of all turns out to be the one I give myself.

The End

Continue the Rebel Journey

Thank you for reading *Rebel Hugger.* Perhaps now you feel inspired and hopeful that you, too, could become so empowered.

You want that feeling of clarity that comes from following the Nudge's wisdom, but aren't sure you know what your own Nudge sounds like.

Let me guide you back to her.

Sign up today to receive the free Connect to Your Nudge Audio Instruction and Worksheet.

Acknowledgments

This book was determined to be written despite me. I felt her calling me forward no matter how many times I had to stop and start over again, nearly from scratch. I would not have made it through this process without the following support:

My book coach, editor extraordinaire, and good friend, Maggie McReynolds. She never gave up on me even when I wanted to give up on myself. She knew what I was capable of and didn't let me settle for anything less, even when the work I shared with her was elementary. She held space for me when I cried and gently urged me to push forward. She was also the one to recognize when I needed to walk away from the work and give myself time to breathe and recover from the intense inner work this book sparked in me. This story is mine, but the finished product is ours.

Ashley started out as a writing buddy over Zoom. We'd meet every Tuesday and write together, keeping us on track with our respective work. In the three years since we started writing together, we've developed a deep friendship that has evolved into supporting each other through all areas of life. I owe her my sanity when the last six months of bringing this book to life tried to take it from me.

Cooper and Parker, my teenage boys, who couldn't care less about this work, but I know they are proud of me. I hope one day this work touches their hearts. They are the living embodiment of my heart outside of my chest.

Kim, my older sister, fierce protector, and greatest cheerleader. She's always there with open arms, ready to catch me when I fall, hold me when I don't have the strength, and smack me back into reality when needed. Her home is where I retreated when things got too heavy.

Bambi, my younger sister, who unconditionally accepts me any way I am. She listens to me patiently when I lie on the floor crying and waits for the perfect moment to make me laugh again. She gets my weird because she's the same kind of weird. She's who I'd call when I got tired of going deep and just wanted to be.

To each and every one of them, I extend my deepest gratitude.

About the Author

Melinda Lee is an adventurous soul who believes in the power of hugs. She wrote her debut memoir, *Rebel Hugger*, as a love letter to herself and all of humanity. She is a certified practitioner of Healing Touch for Animals and BARE coach certified. She uses nature, energy healing, and community to help empower women. She currently resides in Atlanta, Georgia, with her two teenage boys, two mischievous cats, and one exasperated chihuahua.

Rebel Hugger: Reading Group Guide

1. In the opening chapter, Melinda shares her multiple sclerosis diagnosis at twenty-four. Rather than accepting a life of illness, she hears for the first time the still, small voice of the Nudge, an intelligence that directs her to follow a new, relatively unknown healing path. Are you familiar with your own inner intelligence, your Nudge? Have you ever followed its guidance even if it sounded absolutely insane?

2. Melinda is surprised when hugging strangers brings out her own unexpected judgments and prejudices. Can you relate to any of these prejudices? Can you think of times when you've had judgments about people or groups of people that proved to be untrue?

3. Melinda's people-pleasing habit leads to her first experience of feeling unsafe during her Year of Hugs. Do you remember a time when people-pleasing led you to override your instincts and put you in harm's way either emotionally or physically?

4. Melinda notes that while she understood the importance of boundaries for others, she struggled with her own, as shown during a time she felt violated on her cross-country hug trip. In middle school, she writes, she didn't report a teacher for being inappropriate because she knew no one would do anything to protect her. Do you know where your boundaries are? Are you good at enforcing them? Do you feel you have the right to?

5. Melinda learns through a trusted life coach that "I don't know" is a complete answer, which feels like the greatest epiphany of her life. Do you feel like you have to have everything figured out? What's been the greatest advice you've received in your own life?

6. Melinda listens to her own hateful self-talk and is shocked to discover the greatest bully in her life is herself. Take a moment or even few hours to spy on the thoughts in your own brain. What are they saying to you? Are they full of love or judgment?

7. Melinda continues to grapple with feeling unworthy during her cross-country trip and has a hard time receiving all the blessings her hosts offer her. Are you good at receiving from others? Gifts? Compliments? Their time? How does it feel when someone gratefully receives from you? Can the act of receiving be enough of a gift to give back?

8. At one point, Melinda has a severe physical reaction to a topic that comes up over dinner and uses tools she'd learned over the years to calm her nervous system and stay engaged with her dinner guest. What do you do when you find yourself fundamentally dis-

agreeing with someone? Avoid the situation? Fight? Try to find middle ground? Agree to disagree? What would you have done in this situation?

9. By chapter nineteen, Melinda has lost nearly everything that mattered to her—her spouse, best friends, and almost all her worldly possessions. With nothing left to lose, she finds a power within herself to start advocating for her own worth. Do we need to lose it all to find strength we didn't know we had, and if not, how can we discover it without experiencing a complete collapse of everything we think we value? Do you ever reevaluate your possessions, your relationships, or your job to be sure they still hold value for you, or do you keep your head down, afraid to know something needs to change?

10. Melinda writes, "Before I could learn to love others up close, I had to learn to love myself up close." What does loving someone up close, including yourself, mean to you? What does that look like? What does it feel like? Is there anything that keeps you from loving up close?

11. Melinda suggests that unconditional love for self and others requires vulnerability, extreme self-love, and boundaries. Do you agree? Is there anything else you would add to that list?

12. This book is a culmination of everything Melinda learned while hugging thousands of strangers, family, friends. What is your relationship to hugs? Has reading this memoir made you think differently about them? How? Do you feel inspired to hug more—or less?

www.ingramcontent.com/pod-product-compliance
Lightning Source LLC
Chambersburg PA
CBHW021220130626
46554CB00004B/1295